MULTINATIONAL INDUSTRIAL RELATIONS SERIES

No. 4. Latin American Studies
(4b—Mexico)

$37\ell\text{-}2$
44

THE POLITICAL, ECONOMIC, AND LABOR CLIMATE IN MEXICO

by

JAMES L. SCHLAGHECK
Research Assistant
Industrial Research Unit

with the assistance of

NANCY R. JOHNSON and GRACE F. HEMPHILL
Research Assistants
Industrial Research Unit

HD
8116.5
$S34$
1980

INDUSTRIAL RESEARCH UNIT
The Wharton School, Vance Hall/CS
University of Pennsylvania
Philadelphia, Pennsylvania 19104
U.S.A.

186844

Foreword

In 1972, the Industrial Research Unit began an ongoing research project dealing with the international activities of trade unions and the potential for multinational bargaining. This research has resulted in the publication of seven articles, the drafting of others in progress, and work on a book. In addition, a Multinational Information Service has been established based upon the numerous contacts developed in Europe, Asia, Australia, and North and South America; the materials collected are, we believe, the most complete extant on international union and multinational corporation contacts and relationships. The project is under the joint direction of Professor Richard L. Rowan, Co-Director of the Industrial Research Unit, and the undersigned.

A second aspect of this multinational industrial relations research is the translation into the English language of key labor relations and public policy documents. Thus, the Industrial Research Unit has issued English versions of the French "Sudreau Report" (*The Reform of the Enterprise in France*) and of the *German Codetermination Act of May 4, 1976, and Shop Constitution Law of January 15, 1972.*

A third phase of the Industrial Research Unit's multinational industrial relations project is the examination of the labor relations situation and climate in various countries. Studies of Australia, Canada, and the United Kingdom are underway, and studies of a number of Southeastern Asian countries are scheduled to commence early in 1978. This study, *The Political, Economic, and Labor Climate in Mexico,* is both the second of these studies to be published and the second to focus upon a Latin American country. It will be followed by similar ones dealing with Peru, Venezuela, and Colombia.

The Industrial Research Unit also makes special unpublished studies of labor conditions in various countries by request. The Unit's capability in this field has been greatly enhanced as a result of the Chase Manhattan Bank's gift of its international industrial relations library and extensive files. The Chase files, developed over a twelve-year period, are on a country-by-country basis from Abu Dhabi to Zambia. In addition to the industrialized countries, these files also include materials on all underdeveloped areas, with extensive coverage of current industrial relations developments, legislation, labor conditions, policies, and practices. These complement the Industrial Research Unit's already extensive materials on companies and unions.

The author of this study, James L. Schlagheck, did his undergraduate studies at Georgetown University and also studied at the Getulio Vargas Foundation and at Pontificia Universidade Catolica in Rio de Janeiro. He is proficient in Portuguese, Spanish, and French and worked for two major United States corporations for several years in Brazil. He completed his requirements for the Master of Business Administration degree in the Graduate Division of the Wharton School in May 1977. He was also the author of our first study in this series, dealing with Brazil. He is now employed by a major American financial institution. He was assisted in the final stages of the work by Nancy R. Johnson, who was awarded her M.B.A. degree from Wharton in May 1978 and whose work on Peru was published in 1978, and by Lois A. Rappaport, Senior Research Specialist in Multinational Studies. The report on developments from 1977 to 1980 was written by Grace F. Hemphill, currently an M.B.A. candidate.

Robert E. Bolick, Jr., Chief Editor of the Industrial Research Unit, edited the manuscript and made up the index. Margaret E. Doyle, Office Manager, handled the various administrative matters involved in the work, and Mary McCutcheon typed the manuscript. The study was financed by the contributions of our Multinational Research Advisory Group Members and Information Service Subscribers. Such funds are unrestricted, although it is understood that they will be used for multinational industrial relations studies. The authors are, of course, solely responsible for the study's content and for the research and views expressed, which should not be attributed to the University of Pennsylvania.

HERBERT R. NORTHRUP, *Director*
Industrial Research Unit
The Wharton School
University of Pennsylvania

Philadelphia
November 1979

TABLE OF CONTENTS

Table of Contents vii

LIST OF TABLES

LIST OF FIGURES

ILLUSTRATION

MEXICO

x

CHAPTER I

Introduction

Mexico's history of political stability and labor relations is unique among most Latin American countries. For forty-seven years, a dominant-party political system that is closely allied with organized labor has governed the country without military interventions, major revisions of the constitution, or serious contest. Indeed, this stability has been a prime attraction for foreign investment. "Financial responsibility," Mexico's government has proclaimed, "is a hallmark of stable government. That, in turn, is precisely why foreign investment in Mexico continues to grow." [1]

In this study, we shall investigate Mexico's foreign investment climate, focusing specifically on the country's labor environment and the prominent role which Mexican labor groups have come to exercise in national politics and the economy. Mexico's economic development, we shall see, is showing signs of malaise. As the 1976 devaluations of the peso after twenty-two years of fixed parity to the dollar make clear, the country's continued prosperity may well depend on "less stable" financial policies and on tighter controls on inflation, imports, and foreign debt. The political regime in Mexico is therefore in somewhat of a delicate situation. The government can either maintain its close rapport with labor at the likely expense of higher wages and continued inflation, or it can toughen its stand on wage increases to correct distortions in the economy at the likely expense of its broad labor support. Either option can have a serious impact on Mexico's economic progress and political stability.

For the multinational businessman interested in investing or expanding operations in Mexico, the pressing question is, Can Mexico continue its record of political stability and economic growth? The following overviews of the current status of Mexico's political system, economy, and, specifically, labor organiza-

---

[1] Director General de Informacion, "Mexico, Today and Tomorrow," advertisement, *Wall Street Journal*, September 7, 1976, p. 9.

TABLE I-1
A Thumbnail Description of Mexico's Demography, Politics,
Economy, and Labor Force

Area	764,000 square miles (approximately eight times larger than West Germany or one-fourth the size of the continental United States).
Population	61,000,000 (1977 estimate). Mexico's population is approximately 63 percent urban-centered; 46.4 percent of the population is under 15 years of age.
Major Cities	Mexico City (10,490,000), Guadalajara (1,800,000), Monterrey (1,500,000), Ciudad Juarez (490,000), Leon (460,000), and Puebla (450,000).
Political Regime	Dominant-party system: various parties exist, but one, the PRI, virtually controls the governing process. Thirty-one states comprise Mexico's political-administrative network.
Economic Growth	The 1971-1975 average annual GNP growth rate was 5.6 percent. Annual per capital income is US$990 (1975 estimate).
Trade	Exports—US$1.2 billion (1976): oil, sugar, coffee, minerals, steel, manufactured goods. Imports—US$2.4 billion (1976): mechanical and electrical equipment, chemical raw materials, automobile parts, cereals, and seed.
Inflation	17 percent in 1975. Price controls are used to restrain the nation's inflationary propensity.
Labor Force	16.5 million workers currently comprise the Mexican work force; the effective unemployment rate is estimated at 17 percent.
Official Exchange Rate	US$1 = 28.88 Pesos (in August 1976, Mexico converted to a free-floating exchange quotation).

tions provide vital information for a better understanding of Mexico's investment climate as a whole.

Whenever possible, footnotes are provided to substantiate the data presented throughout this study. Some of the information which follows, however, is the product of the author's conversations with international labor specialists and businessmen knowledgeable of the region, correspondence with Latin American unionists, as well as personal insight. Regrettably, not all of these latter sources can be duly acknowledged in this text.

CHAPTER II

Politics In Mexico

The politics, economy, and society of modern day Mexico have deep roots in the Mexican Revolution of 1910. To understand contemporary Mexico, a brief review of the causes and impact of that great upheaval is essential.

THE MEXICAN REVOLUTION OF 1910

By the turn of this century, Mexico was a republic which had emerged from Spanish colonialism and moved through years of political strife into a harsh dictatorship under Porfirio Diaz. Under the strict rule of Diaz, Mexico's agricultural and industrial sectors became particularly oligopolistic and oppressive. Most of the nation's land, for example, was broken down into *haciendas*—large farms nearly self-sufficient in production and practically self-governing—which were owned by only 830 families or corporations during the Diaz period.[1] Only a miniscule middle class existed in the country. The vast part of Mexico's population groveled to make a living from subsistence tenant farming or factory work.

The Diaz government did encourage industrialization, but severely polarized Mexican society between the small, landowning elite and Mexico's large, impoverished, and increasingly hostile peasant and working classes:

> If, on one hand, [the Diaz regime] accelerated industrialization, on the other hand it blocked attempts to promote trade unionism, hired bandits as its police force to suppress peasant revolts, encouraged the entry of foreign capital, usurped property, and instituted a rule of the privileged.[2]

---

[1] U.S. Department of Labor, *Labor Law and Practice in Mexico*, BLS Report No. 240 (Washington, D.C.: U.S. Government Printing Office, 1963), p. 5; and Thomas E. Weil *et al.*, *Area Handbook for Mexico*, 2nd ed. (Washington, D.C.: U.S. Government Printing Office, 1975) p. 293.

[2] *Imagem do Brasil e da America Latina* (Sao Paulo: Editora Banas S.A., 1975), p. 54. Unless otherwise noted, all translations are by the author.

3

Thus, class tensions in Mexico escalated. Bitter clashes over landownership erupted throughout the country, followed by violent government reprisals. Labor organizations and strikes were ruthlessly suppressed. By November 1910, Mexico's drastic social and economic problems exploded in a bloody revolution and civil war.

It is especially significant that Mexican labor "contributed considerably to the development of . . . discontent against the Diaz regime." [3] Indeed, labor had a conspicuous part in fomenting the 1910 uprising. The Cananea miners' strike is a case in point:

> The miners of Cananea [a large copper mine in Northern Mexico] played a historic role in the Mexican Revolution when on May 28, 1906 they started a strike against the American owners . . . which was brutally defeated with the use of troops from across the nearby border and the killing of hundreds of strikers and their families.
>
> The resultant uproar against . . . the dictator Porfirio Diaz, who approved the authorization of the foreign troops, was a strong element in building a national movement that finally overthrew him in 1910. The copper miners' strike at Cananea, along with that of the textile workers of Rio Branco that same year, became the historic take-off point of the workers' movement and the social revolution in modern Mexico.[4]

By rallying workers and peasants against the Diaz government, then, labor won a place for itself in Mexican history as a champion of the Mexican Revolution. As will be shown throughout this study, this fact is a vital factor underlying Mexico's current business climate.

The 1910 Revolution and civil war was to cost Mexico one million lives and to last effectively some ten years, completely reshaping the country's social, economic, and political life. Because of organized labor's historic role in the Revolution, unions gained socially the respect of the Mexican people and their political institutions. This deep respect is still very much prevalent in Mexico today. As one United States government official who worked in Mexico for a number of years pointed out, "Mexican organized labor is a highly respected element of Mexican society

---

[3] Robert J. Alexander, *Organized Labor in Latin America* (New York: The Free Press, 1965), p. 185.

[4] "Mexican Government Acquires Control of Anaconda," *Metal, Bulletin of the International Metalworkers' Federation*, Vol. XI (August-December 1971), p. 2. The important role of the Cananea strike in the Mexican Revolution is mentioned in Alexander, *Organized Labor*, pp. 184-185.

because of labor's prominent role in the Revolution and, even today, in the political process of the country. When the red and black [strike] flag goes up, everyone respects it." [5]

Economically, the emergence of small "leased farms" (*ejidos*) and of a sizeable middle class are also heritages of the 1910 Revolution. Although Mexican politicians are still grappling with the problem of agrarian reform, the fundamental cause of Mexico's revolt, the Revolution did rid the country of most of its aristocratic landowning elite. Today, Mexico's landholding system includes some large private farms, many small individual ones, cooperatives, as well as the *ejidos*. It should be pointed out, however, that

> Most of the *ejidos* are on land distributed by the government from federal holdings or expropriated private property. Although the *ejido* is a legal entity and the land is held jointly, it is generally divided into family plots farmed by individual *ejidatarios* (*ejido* members) who receive the profits. *Ejidatarios* may not legally sell or mortgage the land, although their rights to it may be passed on to their heirs. Since the individual plots are small and therefore generally unsuitable for mechanization or efficient methods of cultivation, they usually provide no more than a bare subsistence level of living. [6]

A few large landholders still do exist in Mexico, although their number and power are greatly reduced since the Revolution. In their place, Mexico's industrialization and revolutionary movements together created a wealthy group of entrepreneurs and businessmen who have risen to prominent positions in Mexican society. One of the major changes sparked by the Revolution, in fact, has been "the development of a rapidly growing middle-income class which, at the top, merges with the upper-income group." [7] This middle class is an important and mobile segment of modern Mexico's economy.

On the political side, Mexico's Revolution gave rise to an intensely nationalist sentiment, a new constitution, and a dominant-party political system. The latter two outcomes are closely tied to Mexican labor and are of critical importance. When the 1910 revolt against the Diaz government lapsed into civil war under Pancho Villa, Emiliano Zapata, and other revolutionary

---

[5] Thomas E. Walsh, Labor Attaché to Mexico, interview held in Washington, D.C., May 14, 1976.

[6] U.S. Department of Labor, *Labor Law and Practice in Mexico*, p. 5.

[7] *Ibid.*, p. 16.

figures, a new constitution was promulgated in 1917 affirming the social equality of all Mexicans to pave the way for agrarian reform and national unity. That constitution, still in effect today, provides for a democratic, federal, and republican form of government. Moreover, one of the constitution's "most important . . . guarantees which relate to land, labor and social welfare is article 123 dealing with labor protection." [8] In other words, Mexico's basic government charter—the Constitution of 1917—institutionalizes a strong political concern for labor.

Perhaps the most noteworthy consequence of Mexico's Revolution, however, is the emergence of a dominant-party governing system that is closely allied with the Mexican labor movement. Mexico's Revolutionary Party—the group which politically spearheaded resistance to the Diaz government—"continues to be the most important political force in the nation" despite various changes of name and a number of reorganizations.[9] Known today as the *Partido Revolucionario Institucional,* or the PRI, this single party has elected all of Mexico's presidents for the past forty-seven years. It has done so, it must be emphasized, with the support and participation of Mexico's main labor organizations. According to Latin American labor scholar Robert J. Alexander:

> Because of the affiliation of most of the labor movement with the government political party [the PRI], a particularly reciprocal relationship has existed between the administration and the trade unions for most of the history of Mexican organized labor.
>
> .   .   .   .
>
> . . . *The country's most important labor leaders are in a very real sense members of the small group which in fact governs Mexico.*[10] (Italics added.)

Clearly, the Revolution of 1910 has had a series of critical effects. Close political-labor ties have developed in its wake. In fact, recent Mexican presidents have gone on record extending their "cordial, affectionate, and solidaristic regards to all workers," assuring Mexico's labor force that "the President of the Republic is attentive to your quests, demands and petitions

---

[8] *Ibid.,* p 24.

[9] U.S. Department of State, *Background Notes: Mexico* (Washington, D.C.: U.S. Government Printing Office, 1975), p. 3.

[10] Alexander, *Organized Labor,* p. 197.

with revolutionary conviction." [11] But despite these ties and the fact that Mexicans believe their Revolution to be an ongoing process, many of the express objectives of Mexico's Revolution have never been fully accomplished. This fact lurks behind the real stability of Mexico's political system. When swarms of Mexican peasants invaded large private farms to lay claim to their own parcels of land prior to the 1976 change of administrations, one Latin American publication remarked, "Day by day the clamor of discontent grows in that the Mexican Revolution, which cost one million lives and is now 66 years old, has yet to finally accomplish its fundamental agrarian objectives." [12]

MEXICO'S CURRENT POLITICAL SYSTEM

The "ongoing" Revolution of 1910, the Constitution of 1917, the Institutional Revolutionary Party or PRI, and organized labor are the four mainstays of Mexico's government process at the present time. An overview of the current political system in Mexico is provided in Table II-1.

It has already been pointed out that the Institutional Revolutionary Party, the PRI, continues overwhelmingly to dominate Mexican politics, and that labor elements play a key part in the party. Since 1929, the PRI has consistently elected all of Mexico's presidents, all of the country's congressmen, and virtually all state officials. In the 1976 elections, in fact, the PRI was the only registered party even to nominate a presidential candidate. [13] These facts have brought some observers to suggest that the PRI is not an ideological party in the traditional sense, but that, instead, it functions "as a Ministry of Elections for the self-perpetuating political bureaucracy." [14] Today, the "self-perpetuating" propensity of the PRI stems from the broad support which the party derives from three critical sources, of which organized labor is undoubtedly the most important:

---

[11] Luis Echeverría Álvarez, "Mensaje a la classe obrera," speech delivered to an assembly of labor representatives on February 27, 1971; reprinted in *El Gobierno Mexicano* (Mexico, D.F.: Presidencia de la República, 28 Febrero 1971).

[12] "Elección asegurada," *Vision: La Revista Interamericana*, 1 Julio 1976, p. 13.

[13] A synopsis of the 1976 presidential election in Mexico is provided in Alan Riding, "Why the Vote Still Counts," *Financial Times*, June 30, 1976, p. 4.

[14] *Ibid.*

TABLE II-1
A Profile of Mexico's Current Political Organization

Administration	Government system is federal and republican, based on the Constitution of 1917 and the principle of separate executive, legislative, and judicial powers.
	Thirty-one states and a federal district comprise the country's administrative network.
	Power not vested in the federal government is reserved for the states; in practice, however, Mexican state governments have less power than their United States counterparts.
Parties	Dominant faction is Mexico's Institutional Revolutionary Party (PRI), the "official party" which controls the government mechanism with close labor support.
	Opposition parties include the moderately conservative, pro-Catholic National Action Party (*Partido de Acción Nacional*—PAN); the centrist Authentic Revolutionary Party (*Partido Autentico de la Revolución Mexicana* —PARM); and the Marxist Popular Socialist Party (*Partido Popular Socialista*—PPS).
	Mexico's Communist Party (*Partido Comunista de México*—PCM) lacks the membership required for official electoral registration and therefore does not participate in Mexico's elections.
	All parties maintain ties with Mexico's various labor organizations.
Executive	Mexico's president, elected to a single 6-year term, dominates the governing process; there is no vice-president in the Mexican system.
	The president executes congressionally-enacted laws, but has direct legislative authority in financial and economic matters.
	The current president is Jóse López Portillo (1976-1982).
Legislative	Bicameral system: 64 senators (two from each state) are elected to 6-year terms; some 200 deputies (Lower House) serve 3-year terms and are elected on a proportionally representative basis.
	Mexico's "one party system"—*i.e.*, the preeminence of the PRI in the presidency and Congress—strongly enhances the power of Mexico's president of that of its Congress. Congress rarely overrides a presidential veto in Mexico.
	Unlike the United States practice, Mexican voters elect a full slate of candidates to fill both Houses of Congress on a nonstaggered basis.

TABLE II-1—Continued

Judicial	A Supreme Court and federal and local court systems adjudicate constitutional and civil disputes.
	Mexico's legal system incorporates a special feature known as *amparo* by which any individual may challenge judicial and legislative acts on the ground that they violate individual guarantees provided by the Constitution.
	Labor Court decisions may be appealed only to the Supreme Court and then only if individual rights are alleged to have been infringed upon.

Sources: U.S. Department of State, *Background Notes: Mexico* (Washington, D.C.: U.S. Government Printing Office, 1975); Martha Lowenstern, *Foreign Labor Information—Labor in Mexico* (Washington, D.C.: U.S. Bureau of Labor Statistics, 1958); Robert Spiets Benjamin, "Mexico's Elections Emphasize Nation's Political Stability," advertisement of the Mexican government, *New York Times*, July 9, 1975, p. A-7; and *Constitución Política de los Estados Unidos Mexicanos.*

Membership in the PRI is on a group basis and all groups are organized into three broad sectors—labor, agrarian, and popular—from which candidates for elective offices are selected. The labor sector, which represents organized labor, is dominated by . . . the Confederation of Mexican Workers (CTM) [*Confederación de Trabajadores de México*, Mexico's largest labor confederation], although most other labor organizations are also represented within the PRI. The organized farmers, largely the more than 2.5 million *ejidatarios*, are represented in the agrarian sector through the National Farmers' Confederation (*Confederación Nacional Campesina*—CNC) and two much smaller and less influential organizations. . . . The third sector, the popular sector, includes groups not in the other two. The strongest group is the well-organized Federation of Government Workers' Unions (*Federación de Sindicatos de Trabajadores al Servicio del Estado*—FSTSE), which is prohibited by party organization from belonging to the labor sector.[15]

Thus, organized labor groups exert a very strong influence on Mexico's government via the PRI, a fact which once prompted one American union official to remark with some exaggeration that Mexico's presidents are "elected by organized labor, and only organized labor."[16] According to at least one United States

---

[15] U.S. Department of Labor, *Labor Law and Practice in Mexico*, p. 18.

[16] Comment made by the American Federation of Labor's Robert Haberman in 1924, quoted in Harvey A. Levenstein, *Labor Organizations in the United States and Mexico* (Westport, Conn.: Greenwood Publishing Co., 1971), p.

government handbook on Mexico, it is a fact that "rewards to labor leadership for cooperation with the government are abundant. CTM leaders, for example, have held seats in the National Congress on a regular basis for thirty years." [17]

Other political parties exist in Mexico today and have also cultivated labor ties, but their political voices are very weak (see Table II-1). The former head of Mexico's Popular Socialist Party (*Partido Popular Socialista*—PPS), Vincente Lombardo Toledano, developed his party's ties with local Marxist labor organizations and also served as secretary general of the communist WFTU (World Federation of Trade Unions). [18] Mexico's second largest party, the National Action Party (*Partido de Acción Nacional*—PAN), is led largely by business and professional men who are working to extend their labor support, as is the centrist Authentic Revolutionary Party (*Partido Autentico de la Revolución Mexicana*—PARM). It is significant, however, that the Popular Socialist and Authentic Revolutionary Parties both endorsed the 1976 PRI presidential candidate—today, President José López Portillo—in Mexico's most recent elections.

A shift that is taking place in Mexican politics with the recent changeover to the Portillo administration is also worthy of note. Mexico's former President Luis Echeverría Álvarez, who left office in December 1976, has been described as a leader who "espoused the full rhetoric and some of the policies of the further left, and sought to be a leader of the economically disenfranchised third world." [19] During Echeverría's mandate, ambitious socially-minded spending programs were implemented, Mexico's foreign debt soared, and consistent government attempts to placate the labor sector came to startle foreign investors as well as the country's middle class. In the words of one resident, 'Echeverría dealt confidence a final blow in his last weeks by attacking businessmen in the industrial centre of Monterrey as "Sunday Christians with no social conscience, defrauding the people after

---

110. Although the quotation is both dated and overstated, it nevertheless suggests the vital role which organized labor has played and continues to play in Mexican politics.

[17] Weil *et al.*, *Area Handbook*, p. 230.

[18] U.S. Department of Labor, *Labor Law and Practice in Mexico*, p. 15.

[19] Dalton Robertson, "Plain Man's Guide to What You Should Know about Mexico," *Financial Post*, February 19, 1977, p. 7.

•

leaving Mass," and by suddenly nationalizing huge acres of rich farmland in the Sonora [Northwestern] area.'[20]

Current President José López Portillo, Mexico's uncontested presidential heir, came into office via the PRI machine after Echeverría and inherited the party's broad policies and support bases. As will be shown in subsequent sections of this study, Mexico's new president inherited a series of critical economic problems as well. But so far, Portillo's policies and statements are far removed from the militant nationalism and latent anti-big business, antimultinational enterprise posture of the Echeverría government. Portillo, a conservative lawyer and former Finance Minister, has instead affirmed, "We do not want the present situation to make us lose our way or our structure by forcing us, as have been others, to extremes."[21] As one observer more directly described the change in Mexico's political stance:

> By the pendulum theory of Mexican politics, Portillo should be the president to reassure business, undo the alienation of the local private sector, and encourage foreign investment within the parameters of what's possible in Mexico.[22]

THE POLITICAL FUTURE

Thus far, Mexico's record of political stability is unparalleled among most Latin American nations. By drawing support from closely allied labor, agrarian, and popular factions, the country's dominant-party system has ruled for several decades without interruption. As one area analyst put it, "One of the secrets of its longevity is the system's basic—though often slow—responsiveness to popular sentiment, without which the myths of revolution, agrarian reform and, now, social democracy, could not be sustained."[23]

Three trends are gaining momentum in Mexico which cast some doubt on the country's political future. They are (1) a growing disillusionment with the government's ability to resolve Mexico's agrarian and economic problems; (2) the escalation of

---

[20] *Ibid.*

[21] "Address to the U.S. Congress by Jose Lopez Portillo, President of Mexico," advertisement of the Mexican government, *Wall Street Journal,* February 18, 1977, p. 9.

[22] Robertson, "Plain Man's Guide," p. 7.

[23] Riding, "Why the Vote Still Counts," p. 4.

political corruption and terrorism in the country; and (3) the gradual erosion of the PRI's broad public support. Subsequent sections of this study will explore the facts underlying the economic and labor components of these trends in greater detail. It suffices to point out here that public confidence in Mexico's monolithic political system appears to be declining, and that the country's dominant-party system has so far been unable to abate its popularity loss. The *Wall Street Journal,* for example, has pointed out:

> For years, land reform has been Mexico's most emotional political issue; the promise of a plot for every peasant ignited the 1910 revolution and has helped sustain loyalty to the country's one-party government ever since. But the pressure it puts on the new administration is intense. As one veteran Mexico-watcher says, "If Lopez Portillo can't restore confidence in the government's ability to solve the agricultural problem, he can't last six years—the length of his term." [24]

At the same time, urban guerrilla raids and violent student protests have escalated in Mexico to the point that Latin American publications now speak of "what appears to be the beginning of a wave of violence" perpetrated by fragmented, radical groups in the country.[25] Mexico's universities are the scene of many such disturbances. In February 1977, for example, a year-old conflict between university leftists and local conservatives in the southern state of Oaxaca boiled over, leading to thirty-six deaths and the overthrow of the state governor. According to one source:

> Part of the conflict stemmed from involvement by leftist students in labor and peasant organizations. But Oaxaca business interests, supported by the governor and his police, also sought to intervene directly at the state university, which is nominally autonomous. . . . There are analogous situations in the state universities of Nayarit and Zacatecas, Guerrero and Sinaloa.[26]

At the National Autonomous University in Mexico City, Dr. Guillermo Soberón, the school's conservative rector, is currently being challenged by the Mexican Communist Party, which has en-

---

[24] John Huey, "Agrarian Reform Fight Riles Mexican Farmers and Hurts Production," *Wall Street Journal,* February 24, 1977, p. 1.

[25] "Elección asegurada," *Vision: La Revista Interamericana,* 1 Julio 1976, p. 12. Mexican terrorist activities and reports of student riots have also been documented in the *New York Times,* August 12, 1976, p. C-62; and in Weil *et al., Area Handbook,* pp. 346-350.

[26] "Strife Engulfs Mexican Campuses," *New York Times,* April 13, 1977, p. B-5.

listed 20,000 academic and administrative employees in a single trade union. That union, press reports have disclosed, is "threatening to close the university." [27]

It is likely that these kinds of confrontations will escalate in Mexico over the next seven years and will weaken the public's support of the PRI government. Moreover, corruption is particularly widespread in Mexico. It is also taking its toll on the public's confidence:

> Perhaps more than any other Latin American country, corruption in Mexico extends from the top levels of government and business down to traffic policemen and customs officials. . . . "For ordinary people, the sight of officials [e]merging with a fortune after six years in government is a source of deep social irritation," a close aide to President Eacheverría said. . . . "The public morals have been steadily worsening and the loss of people's faith in the Government comes partly from the corruption." [28]

For these reasons, interest groups and—it will be shown later in this study—labor groups, in particular, have become increasingly critical of Mexico's government. Public support of the PRI is dropping as a result. Indeed, the PRI's share of the total votes cast in past congressional elections slid from 61.6 percent in 1961 to 45 percent in 1973. [29] The party won only 1,254,900 votes in Mexico City during the 1973 congressional elections versus 1,145,700 votes for the opposition and a large 439,400 invalidated votes. This erosion of PRI support is particularly significant in that considerable support is traditionally mustered by Mexico's main labor confederation, the Mexican Workers' Confederation (*Confederación de Trabajadores de México—* CTM) whose leader, Fidel Velázquez, is also a key PRI figurehead. But as we shall see, even the CTM and other labor organizations are increasingly coming to odds with the government over its wage and development policies. There is considerable

---

[27] *Ibid.*

[28] Alan Riding, "Corruption Again Election Issue in Mexico," *New York Times,* June 29, 1976, p. A-2.

[29] Data on Mexico's 1976 elections are not as yet available. The above statistics on the country's 1973 election returns were taken from Riding, "Why the Vote Still Counts," p. 4. Readers interested in additional information on Mexican politics prior to the Portillo election in 1976 may refer to that detailed article as well as to Evelyn P. Stevens, *Protest and Response in Mexico* (Cambridge, Mass.: The MIT Press, 1974).

evidence, in fact, that labor's support of the PRI may be on the wane, and that traditional labor leaders such as Velázquez are losing their ability to keep the rank and file within the PRI fold.

One important conclusion is that continued PRI rule in Mexico hinges on the ability of the new administration to rebuild its coalition of labor, agrarian, and popular support bases. The task ahead is a difficult one. Indeed, it is possible that a split will occur within the PRI—caused possibly by leftist, Echeverría-supporting factions—which will form a new political group in the country. As this study will now attempt to make clearer, Mexico's political stability may, in fact, be short-lived in the future should the dominant PRI party lose the critical endorsement of organized labor.

CHAPTER III

The Mexican Economy in Profile

INFRASTRUCTURE

Mexico's economy boasts a well-rounded infrastructure which has enabled the country to make significant economic gains since the Revolution. Some sectors of the economy, however—notably agriculture—are still inefficient and problematic. In this section, the main sectors of Mexico's economy are reviewed; the strengths and weaknesses of each, highlighted; and a profile of the status of Mexico's economic development is provided.

Transportation and Port Facilities

Mexico's transportation network is one of the most advanced in Latin America.[1] The country's highway system has more than doubled since 1970 and now comprises more than 111,000 miles or 185,000 kilometers of paved roads, including a portion of the Inter-American Highway which connects Mexico to North, South, and Central America. Major highways provide surface access to virtually all parts of the country, linking most Mexican towns with Mexico City, Guadalajara, and Monterrey. In 1975 alone, about 7.3 billion pesos (US$584 million in 1975 US dollars) were spent on highway and road expansion, a good indication of the priority which good roads and highways are given by the federal government.

---

[1] Information on Mexico's transportation and port facilities was taken from the following sources: Director General de Informacion, "Mexico, Today and Tomorrow," advertisement, *Wall Street Journal*, September 7, 1976, p. 9; U.S. Department of State, *Background Notes: Mexico* (Washington, D.C.: U.S. Government Printing Office, 1975), p. 5; Luis Echeverría Álvarez, *Quinto Informe de Gobierno* (Mexico: Presidencia de la República, 1975), pp. 27-29; *Imagem do Brasil e da America Latina* (Sao Paulo: Editora Banas S.A., 1975), p. 56; The World Bank, *El Grupo del Banco Mundial en las Americas* (Washington, D.C.: The World Bank, 1974), pp. 80-81; and Thomas E. Weil *et al.*, *Area Handbook for Mexico*, 2nd ed. (Washington, D.C.: U.S. Government Printing Office, 1975), pp. 323-330.

Railroads are a second critical means of surface transportation in the country, extending some 15,000 miles or 24,000 kilometers —roughly six times the distance between London and Teheran. Some 26,500 freight cars and 2,000 passenger cars are currently in service in Mexico, with 80 percent of all railway traffic being provided by the government-run National Railways of Mexico. The country also boasts a highly sophisticated air transport network as well. Many international airlines and several domestic ones service Mexico's larger urban centers and link its principal airports to Central and South America, Europe, and the United States. AeroMéxico, the government airline, connects fifty-six local cities and sixteen foreign ones, using one of Latin America's most sophisticated, computerized reservation systems. The airline served 3.4 million passengers in 1975.

Mexico's port facilities, however, have been slow to evolve despite massive injections of federal capital to facilitate better Mexican sea traffic. Mexico has forty-nine ports, five of which— Guaymas, Manzanillo, and Mazatlán on the Pacific; Tampico and Veracruz on the Gulf of Mexico—handle 80 percent of the country's maritime traffic (excluding petroleum shipments). In 1975, some one billion pesos (US$8 million in 1975 US dollars) were allocated for the improvement of these and other national ports.

Communications

Mexico's telecommunications network is also highly developed and interlinks most urban centers and rural areas.[2] Some 2.8 million telephone units are now installed in the country, extending telephone service to 2,973 Mexican cities. Ninety-seven percent of this service is provided by the government-owned Teléfonos de México, which is now giving priority to the extension of telephone service to Huicot, Altos Chiapas, Rio Candelaria, and other rural areas.

In addition, there are 654 radio stations and 162 television stations in operation, facts which point out the degree of sophistication which has been attained in the field of telecommunications. A major component of the country's communications system is a gigantic satellite ground station built in the late 1960s in Tulancingo, Hidalgo. The Hidalgo complex gives Mexico direct tele-

---

[2] Readers desiring further data on Mexico's communications network may refer to: Echeverría Álvarez, *Quinto Informe de Gobierno*, pp. 27-29; *Imagem do Brasil e da America Latina*, p. 56; "Mexico—The Echeverría Years: 1970-1976," advertisement of the Mexican government, *Business Week*, August 16, 1976, p. 27; and Weil *et al.*, *Area Handbook*, pp. 241-258.

phone, telex, and television linkage via satellite with Europe and the rest of Latin America. Since its construction, investment in both the transportation and communications sectors soared 363 percent between 1971 and 1976—from US$367 million to US$1.7 billion. These investments have helped to make Mexico's telecommunications network "one of the most complex and advanced mass communication systems in Latin America." [3]

Energy and Fuel Resources

According to one United States business publication, López Portillo has "several potential solutions to Mexico's economic difficulties. One [of them] is oil." [4] The fact is that since 1974, Mexican oil discoveries in Baja California, Chiapas, and Tabasco have enabled the country to become self-sufficient in crude oil as well as to export crude to Brazil, Israel, Colombia, and the United States. Under the management of a state monopoly, Petróleos Mexicanos (PEMEX), Mexico's petroleum industry has averaged an annual growth rate of 8.6 percent over the past five years. PEMEX currently produces 895,000 barrels of crude each day, and the director of that state agency, Jorge Díaz Serrano, has gone on record affirming that Mexico's ' "probable" petroleum reserves are "far superior" to 60 bn. barrels.' [5] With that amount, Mexico would have at least twice the gas and petroleum of the United States, and some United States officials have speculated that Mexico's Chiapas and Tabasco finds might indeed "be as rich in petroleum as the Persian Gulf." [6]

At the present time, Mexico has some 310 oil wells on line, a sophisticated petroleum storage and distribution system linking Mexico City, Salamanca and Guadalajara, and refineries operating in Salamanca, Manatitlan, and Ciudad Madero. Mexico's refining capacity is limited, but PEMEX recently announced a

---

[3] Weil *et al., Area Handbook,* p. 241.

[4] "Latin America Opens the Door to Foreign Investment Again," *Business Week,* August 9, 1976, p. 38.

[5] "Mexican Oil Reserves 'Far Superior' to 60 bn. Barrels," *Financial Times,* February 23, 1977, p. 5. Information on Mexico's status in petroleum and electricity was also taken from Robert Spiets Benjamin, "Mexico's Elections Emphasize Nation's Political Stability," advertisement of the Mexican government, *New York Times,* July 9, 1976, p. A-7; and *Mexico,* Economist Intelligence Unit Quarterly Economic Review No. 3 (London: EIU, 1976), pp. 8-10.

[6] Lester A. Sobel, ed., *Latin America 1974* (New York: Facts on File, Inc., 1975), p. 130.

six-year, US$15 billion investment program to speed up crude production as well as to enlarge the nation's refinery installations.[7] As one company official put it, ' "PEMEX will be as big as Venezuela is now—in terms of production and reserves" ' by the 1980s.[8] The optimistic, but very possible, implication is that Mexico should be able to strengthen significantly its economy by 1982 with oil exports. According to former President Echeverría, "The critical attention being given to Mexico's vital petroleum capacity at a time of world-wide energy crises guarantees us adequate resources to advance our own, independent, national development." [9] Toward this end, Mexico has sought observer status in the Organization of Petroleum Exporting Countries (OPEC) and sells its oil abroad at OPEC prices (see Table III-1).

Mexico's energy-generating capacity has more than doubled since 1970. The country claims a current output of 14 million kilowatts of electrical power, and its electrical output grew 8.2 percent in 1976. Federal priorities now aim at extending electric service to more of the country's rural areas, and in 1975 some 10 billion pesos (US$800 million in 1975 US dollars) were spent toward this end. At the present time, Mexico leads all Latin American nations in kilowatt capacity and services the electrical energy needs of more than 10,000 villages and urban centers. Sixty percent of the country's kilowatt power is used by industry, however; therefore, continued production growth is a priority being given special attention by federal officials for a stronger national infrastructure. Thus, Mexico's hydroelectric dams and thermoelectric plants in Chicasoasen, Tula, Altamira, and Merida are all slated for expansion and sizeable output increases.[10] New projects call for the construction of twelve addi-

---

[7] "Mexican Oil Reserves 'Far Superior,' " p. 5. PEMEX is reportedly seeking US$720 million in 1976 to finance new growth and to pay interest on its current outstanding debt of US$288 million. "Mexico—The Echeverría Years," p. 35. In March 1977, a syndicate of international financial institutions led by Chase Manhattan, Citicorp, and Westdeutsche Landesbank Gironzentrale organized and signed a $350 million, five-year loan to the company. The Mexican Chamber of Commerce of the United States, Inc., "Monthly Digest," No. 815 (April 1977), p. 13.

[8] "Mexican Oil Reserves 'Far Superior,' " p. 5.

[9] Echeverría Álvarez, *Quinto Informe de Gobierno*, p. 31.

[10] Specific data on the current and projected energy-generating capacities of Mexico's major dams and thermoelectric plants are provided in "Mexico—The Echeverría Years," p. 38.

TABLE III-1
PEMEX Expansion Projects

Product	Capacity (Thousand Tons per year)	Cost (US$ Millions)	Beginning of Production
Ammonium Anhydride	1,490	103	1974-1976
Aromatics	800	40	1977
Ethylene (I)	180	18	1976
Ethylene (II)	500	48	1977
Ethylene Oxide	100	26	1976
High Density Polyethylene (I)	100	33	1976
High Density Polyethylene (II)	100	36	1979
Low Density Polyethylene	180	39	1977
Methanol	150	14	1977
Nitrile Acrylic	50	25	1977
Polypropylene	60	24	1976
Propylene	140	17	1978
Propylene Oxide	40	8	1978

Source: *Imagem do Brasil e da America Latina* (Sao Paulo: Editora Banas S.A., 1975), p. 57.

tional thermoelectric installations by 1982, each with a 300,000 kilowatt generating capacity. The government is also elaborating plans to tap geothermal energy sources and is now constructing a nuclear power plant.

Since hydrocarbon sources of electrical energy account for 90 percent of Mexico's kilowatt output and have become increasingly expensive in the country, the republic's attempts to develop new energy sources, such as nuclear power, are of special significance. Mexico has some 4,300 known tons of uranium reserves, one of the facts which led the government to begin construction of a nuclear power plant in Laguna Verde, Veracruz, in 1971. Mexico is a co-signer of the International Atomic Energy Organization's cooperative agreement which calls for the use of nuclear energy only for the production of electricity. But until Mexico can bring its nuclear power plant on line, over 90 percent of the energy consumed in Mexico will be supplied by the country's petroleum industry.

Mineral Resources

In addition to uranium, other major mineral or mining resources in Mexico include silver, sulphur, lead, zinc, manganese, coal, and iron ore. Mexico is one of the world's largest producers of silver, responsible for some 20 percent of all silver output.[11] It ranks second in the production of bismuth, sulphur, fluorite, and antimony; third in the production of lead. Moreover, Mexican government officials are proud of the fact that their country doubled the value of its mining production between 1970 and 1975, so that the country now has some 2,000 mines, seventy-seven processing plants, and seven smelters in operation. Mineral exports generally represent 10 to 15 percent of Mexico's annual export total; and in 1975, the production of Mexico's mining industry registered a total value of US$1.2 billion.

Even so, Mexico's mining sector has demonstrated unusual growth rates over the last decade. For example, mining production jumped 28 percent from 1972 to 1973, but cumulatively averaged a growth rate of only 3.5 percent per year from 1970 to 1975. This "up-again, down-again" trend has had serious repercussions in Mexico's balance of payments and reflects one of the weaknesses of Mexico's economy. According to local government sources, at least, "a bad year in 1975 saw an eight percent drop in mining production, a 13 percent drop in non-ferrous metals production, and a 4.4 percent drop in iron ore production—a reflection of lower demand by the national steel industry." [12] The government, therefore, is attempting to boost Mexico's steel industry and simultaneously stimulate mining production and export growth. New mining equipment installations in the Florida and Palau mines in the state of Coahuila, for instance, are slated to raise the coal output of each to 1.1 and 1.5 million tons, respectively, in 1977. The past administration also began "government control of the production, administration and trade of sulphur. The policy eventually will be extended to phosphoric rock and potassium." [13] Thus, Mexico's government has begun acquiring equity control of various mineral producers

---

[11] Mexico's ranking among mineral-producing nations is taken from Bruno Pagliai, "The Mining Industry in Mexico," in *Seminar on Doing Business in Modern Mexico*, (Berkeley: University of California at Berkeley, 1967), pp. 6-14. Data on the country's mineral resources are also available in "Mexico—The Echeverría Years," pp. 30 and 39.

[12] "Mexico—The Echeverría Years," p. 30.

[13] *Ibid.*, p. 39.

TABLE III-2

Mexican Production of Selected Metals, 1960-1973

(in metric tons)

	1960	1970	1971	1972	1973
Aluminum	—	33,833	39,932	39,484	39,159
Copper	27,923	60,763	59,718	63,999	61,890
Lead	181,518	170,030	150,555	150,097	166,506
Silver	1,299	1,270	1,054	1,034	1,092
Zinc	84,763	84,585	83,423	83,788	71,423

Source: *Imagem do Brasil e da America Latina*, p. 57.

TABLE III-3

Mexican Production of Selected Metals, 1974 and 1975

	1974		1975	
	Volume (Tons)	Value (US$000)	Volume (Tons)	Value (US$000)
Bismuth	718	12,921	445	6,789
Copper	82,670	175,314	78,196	92,792
Lead	218,021	103,628	178,615	87,165
Mercury	894	7,742	490	2,676
Silver	1,168	178,321	1,183	168,075
Tin	400	3,418	378	2,924
Tungsten	309	2,463	277	2,596
Zinc	262,716	198,026	228,851	196,739

Source: The Mexican Chamber of Commerce of the United States, Inc., "Monthly Digest," No. 816 (May 1977), p. 7.

such as Azufrera Panamericana (APSA), a major sulphur producer and trader, which came under state control in June 1972.

It is also noteworthy that Mexico's constitution defines the country's subsoil and minerals as being the inalienable property of the nation. In accordance with federal mining laws enacted in 1926, 1930, and 1961, all mining activities require a federal concession, and mining companies seeking new concessions from the government must have at least 51 percent of their equity shares in the hands of Mexican citizens. For some minerals such as lead, this "Mexicanization" can go as high as 66 percent.

Agriculture

Efforts to promote the production and export of such crops as coffee, sugar, and cotton have been successful in Mexico in recent years, and the country is largely self-sufficient in most basic foods. Even so, some food imports are still necessary. Furthermore, agriculture continues to be a Pandora's box of serious economic and political problems in modern Mexico.

We have already pointed out that agrarian disputes led to a bloody civil war in Mexico earlier in this century, and that land distribution, the "first phase" of Mexico's post-Revolution agrarian reform, is still a smoldering political issue. ' "There'll be no peace in this country," ' one 62-year-old Mexican peasant was recently quoted, ' "until all the land is distributed to the peasants. . . . When the peasants know there is no more land, then perhaps they won't demand it." ' [14] Mexico's agricultural dilemma—indeed, "the major problem besetting Mexican agriculture," [15]—is that there is a genuine scarcity of arable land. The country's arid climate, harsh topography, irregular rainfalls, and mountain chains limit Mexico's farmland to a mere 16 percent of the total land mass. With 40 percent of the total labor force employed in agriculture, the prospect of equitably dividing Mexico's farmlands among the growing number of peasants would be patently inefficient. Nevertheless, peasant invasions of private land are particularly common with changes of government administrations in Mexico and landownership continues to be a thorny political problem.

Of course, strict constitutional limits have been imposed on the size of private farms since the Revolution. In the case of irrigated land, for instance, a single owner may only hold 250 acres. [16] In 1975, land under irrigation totaled 2.2 million acres, of which 313,690 acres were held in private hands. Most arable land, however, has been expropriated for the establishment of the *ejidos* or small leased farms. As described in the political sec-

---

[14] Alan Riding, "Mexican Peons Vow to Hold Land," *New York Times*, December 9, 1976, p. A-1.

[15] *Imagem do Brasil e da America Latina*, p. 56.

[16] Price Waterhouse & Co., *Doing Business in Mexico* (New York: Price Waterhouse & Co., 1975), p. 17.

tion, the *ejido* plots are generally too small and unsuitable for mechanization; they provide for no more than a subsistence level of farming.

Thus, the second stage of Mexico's agrarian reform—that of raising productivity and living standards in the agricultural sector—has become one of the country's most pressing economic, as well as political, challenges.

The fact is that agriculture, which employs approximately 40 percent of the economically active population, only accounts for 12 percent of Mexico's Gross Domestic Product. Food output has grown only 6.9 percent since 1970, while Mexico's population has grown more than 27 percent from 48 million to some 61 million people. Moreover, three-fourths of Mexico's total crop sales are made by only 15 percent of the country's farmers. The remaining 85 percent produce barely enough for their own consumption on small *ejido* plots of land.[17] With droughts or failing production, thousands of peasants flock to Mexico's urban centers or cross over to the United States in search of gainful employment. Only in Sinaloa and Sonora, two northwestern states in which most arable land is still privately owned and held in large family farms, is agriculture efficient and productive. Peasant wages in both of these states tend to be high, and the availability of work in both is evidenced by the low migration rate from these states to the United States. Even so, the private landowners in Sinaloa and Sonora are enormously wealthy. They have become conspicuous examples of the shortcomings of Mexico's 1910 Revolution.

To address these various problems, former President Echeverría expropriated 220,000 acres of lush Yaqui valley land from private owners in Sonora and distributed them to landless peasants three weeks before leaving office. The expropriation, according to Britain's *Financial Times,* was "one of the most radical and controversial measures of the Echeverría regime."[18] It touched off peasant land seizures and blockades in several neighboring states. As a result, Mexico's production of winter vegetables, most of which is sold in the United States, was virtually paralyzed into 1977.

A federal court ruling under the López Portillo administration annulled the expropriation, and federal troops were dispatched to

---

[17] U.S. Department of State, *Background Notes,* p. 5.

[18] Alan Riding, "Controversial Move," *Financial Times,* November 24, 1976, p. 7.

TABLE III-4

Mexican Production of Selected Agricultural Commodities
(in thousands of metric tons)

	1969	1970	1971	1972	1973
Basic Diet Staples					
Beans	889	1,000	1,000	800	900
Corn	8,596	11,176	9,850	8,926	9,500
Rice	417	399	410	430	450
Sorghum	1,605	2,738	2,200	1,700	1,900
Wheat	2,058	2,262	1,861	1,780	2,000
Other Commodities					
Bananas	986	1,136	1,219	1,280	865
Barley	285	238	305	294	300
Cacao	24	29	29	31	30
Coffee	173	184	192	198	210
Cotton	552	391	322	403	412
Grapes	128	144	219	225	n.a.
Oats	41	63	34	28	55
Oranges	882	940	927	1,650	1,660
Potatoes	377	600	650	680	460 [1]
Soybeans	283	240	250	360	510
Sugar	2,393	2,400	2,402	2,476	2,600
Tobacco	74	69	65	82	65
Tomatoes	675	783	855	950	987 [1]

Source: Weil *et al.*, *Area Handbook*, p. 299.
n.a. not available.
[1] Food and Agriculture Organization estimate.

evict peasants forcibly who were occupying private property in December 1976. These actions, however, embittered Mexico's peasants and many workers as well, rekindling the emotionalism of the country's agrarian problems at the very outset of López Portillo's mandate. In the impassioned words of the head of the General Union of Mexican Workers and Peasants, Juan Rodríguez

Gomez, ' "Those who support . . . [the Sonora] land barons are provoking an armed uprising throughout the nation." ' [19]

To recapitulate, then, the development of Mexican agriculture has been impaired by geography as well as by the creation of leased *ejido* farms which are too small to be efficient. Agriculture is in deep trouble in Mexico. It is an emotionally charged political and economic issue with critical labor implications and a very questionable future. As one observer summarized Mexico's agricultural plight:

> . . . The need to rationalise the "ejido" system is . . . urgent, not only so that increased production will improve the living conditions of the peasantry and reduce imports, but also so that higher productivity will absorb more of the millions of rural underemployed who eventually migrate to the country's overcrowded cities.
>
> The solution apparently chosen [by López Portillo] is the "collective ejido" by which the communal farm would be run as a single economic unit rather than perhaps 400 tiny plots. But there is resistance to the scheme from the peasants themselves who have been brainwashed by six decades of official rhetoric into wanting their own piece of land.[20]

Industry and Manufacturing

The composition of Mexico's Gross Domestic Product (GDP) has changed significantly from the 1960s to the present, the most notable shifts involving industry and manufacturing. Mexican industries produce a wide range of items and supply about 80 percent of all manufactured goods sold in the country. High protective tariffs have helped foster much of Mexico's industrial growth. The industrial sector's share of the GDP increased from 29.2 percent in 1960 to 35.2 percent in 1973. Manufacturing increased its share from 22.6 percent to 27.3 percent during the same period. These changes, according to the Inter-American Development Bank, were largely attributed to "the growth of the domestic market, a long-range import-substitution policy and, in recent years, to the active promotion of industrial exports." [21]

---

[19] "Mexican Seizure of Land Annulled," *New York Times*, December 12, 1976, p. A-14.

[20] Riding, "Controversial Move," p. 7.

[21] Information on the composition of Mexico's GDP and the contributions to it by the industrial and manufacturing sectors was taken from Inter-American Development Bank, *Economic and Social Progress in Latin America: Annual Report 1974* (Washington, D.C.: Inter-American Development Bank, 1974), pp. 345-346.

FIGURE III-1
Mexican Industrial Production

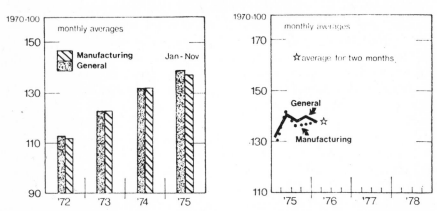

Source: *Mexico*, Economist Intelligence Unit Quarterly Economic Review
Nos. 2 and 3 (London: EIU, 1976), pp. 12 and 10, respectively.

Since the mid-1970s, however, Mexico's advances in output and
industrial growth have become sluggish. Government reports in
1976 related that

> significant growth within the manufacturing industry took place in
> the manufacture of synthetic threads and fibers, their production,
> and trucks. Important increases were achieved in the production
> of automobiles, fertilizers, tires, and inner-tubes, among other prod-
> ucts.[22]

Although Mexico's industrial sector averaged an annual growth
rate of 8.4 percent in the early 1970s, this average had dropped
to 5.3 percent by 1976; for example, manufacturing eked out a
mere 1.9 percent increase in 1976, and the production of capital
goods was down 5 percent that year.[23] What is more, the country's industrial growth average is likely to *remain* at low levels
over the next several years before it can be significantly improved. According to one well-founded analysis of Mexico's industrial sector:

> . . . Inflation and urban . . . unemployment, plus the lack of con-
> sumer credit, have hurt consumer demand. The worst sectors are
> those based on elastic consumer demand and import content, such

----

[22] Benjamin, "Mexico's Elections Emphasize Nation's Political Stability,"
p. A-7.

[23] Inter-American Development Bank, *Economic and Social Progress*, p. 346;
"Mexico—The Echeverría Years," p. 38; The Mexican Chamber of Commerce, Inc., "Monthly Digest," No. 815 (April 1977), p. 5.

as autos, whose sales and production will plummet 25 percent or more [in 1977]. Industrial production as a whole is projected to grow about 2 percent only because of bright spots in petroleum, mining, steel and electrical energy.[24]

We have already highlighted the status of Mexico's energy and fuel resources. The country's steel production, the second largest in Latin America after Brazil's, has doubled since 1970, averaging a 9 percent annual growth rate in recent years. In 1971 and 1972, in fact, Mexico's steel production began exceeding domestic demand, enabling the country to become a steel exporter. In 1973, however, Mexico's steel exports dropped 60 percent in volume and 44 percent in value; steel imports jumped from 258,840 tons (US$83.7 million) in 1972 to 534,730 tons (US$167.7 million) in 1973.[25] By 1976, Mexico's steel industry was operating at near capacity, producing approximately 7 million tons.

Steel is a 45,000-employee industry in Mexico and is comprised of ten major and numerous smaller firms. The largest, Altos Hornos de México, which is primarily a state-owned enterprise, accounts for some 40 percent of Mexico's total steel production.[26] It recently began an expansion program to "raise its capacity to 3.75 million tons of steel a year." [27] Another government-owned steel company at Las Truchas, a $3 billion complex recently begun 460 miles from Mexico City and scheduled for completion in 1977, was to be the largest single industrial investment by the Mexican government. The Las Truchas development program, however, was postponed by the government in mid-1977. Additional commitment to the project, local sources explained, "would severely strain Mexico's balance of payments and require public spending and foreign borrowing well above levels on which agreement was reached recently with the International Monetary Fund." [28] For this reason, the Mexican government subsequently announced plans in May 1977 to merge the operations of the country's three major steel producers—Altos Hornos, Las Truchas, and Fundidora de Hierro & Acero de Monterrey—in an effort to

---

[24] "Business Outlook—Mexico," *Business Latin America*, March 9, 1977, p. 77.

[25] *Imagem do Brasil e da America Latina*, p. 57.

[26] Weil *et al.*, *Area Handbook*, p. 308.

[27] "Mexico—The Echeverría Years," p. 30.

[28] "Mexico Postpones Big Expansion at State-Owned Steel Complex," *New York Times*, April 1, 1977, p. D-9.

boost production and save investment capital. The triumvirate
will be managed by a new state-supervised holding company,
Sidemex. It will, Mexican officials contend, "save the country
$3.5 billion of an estimated $5.1 billion in new investments, most
of it in foreign currency, required over the next three to five
years to make Mexico self-sufficient in steel." [29]

Indeed, this government mobilization has come at a critical
time. As one 1977 steel report out prior to the merger announcement made clear:

> Because of the year-old slump in economic activity here, demand
> for steel has been slack and, with an output of seven million tons
> per year, the steel industry is producing a small surplus for export.
> But unless new steel expansions take place before 1979, many ex-
> perts believe that Mexico will once again become a net steel im-
> porter by 1982.[30]

Of course, a large part of Mexico's projected steel consumption
hinges on local demand for autos and trucks. Numerous vehicle
producers have major operations in Mexico, including Chrysler,
Ford, General Motors, International Harvester, Nissan, Vehiculos
Automotores Mexicanos, Volkswagen, Diesel Nacional, and Mexicana de Autobuses. Sahagún—a state-supported consortium of
eleven tractor, bus, and engine-producing firms—currently employs 17,300 people and produces 30,000 autos, 2,556 railroad
cars, and 36,000 diesel engines annually.[31] These indicators are
expected to increase once Mexico's automobile market grows.

Indeed, there has been notable expansion in Mexico's automobile and vehicle industries, and subcontracting in them has tended
to create more jobs—at least during the early 1970s. But government regulations make many finished automotive products "more
costly than if imported." [32] Each automotive firm's output is also
regulated by federal quotas which may only be increased when a
company demonstrates that its expanded production will result
in export revenues that can offset the cost of any imported parts
needed. Moreover, low consumer demand for autos and trucks is
expected to prevail in 1977 and 1978 because of Mexico's difficult

---

[29] "Mexico Plans to Merge 3 Major Steel Firms in Bid to Boost Output,"
Wall Street Journal, May 12, 1977, p. 8.

[30] "Mexico Postpones Big Expansion at State-Owned Steel Complex," p.
D-9.

[31] "Mexico—The Echeverría Years," p. 31.

[32] Weil *et al.*, *Area Handbook*, p. 309.

economic situation. This will affect steel consumption and add to the pressures restraining the growth of Mexico's industrial sector.

Other major industries in Mexico include those producing or processing food, beverages, apparel, paper and pulp, tobacco (which collectively represent some 30 percent of Mexico's Gross Domestic Product), and construction, which has suffered unsteady growth rates with increases and decreases in federal housing expenditures. In recent months, federal outlays for housing—representing some 70 percent of all construction investment—have been sharply cut back in an attempt to restrain inflation. Mexico's construction industry may thus show even less improvement in 1977 than it showed in 1976 when it registered zero growth. As a result, jobs are more difficult to find for the 730,000 people who were employed in construction in Mexico in the early 1970s. Largely automated and "still hampered by high labor costs," [33] Mexico's 2,000 textile companies in operation and employing approximately 200,000 workers are likewise hiring fewer and fewer workers. Mexico's 750 pharmaceutical firms are expanding output, but only employ 38,000 people.

Thus, technology and productivity—ultimately, industrial growth and employment—are pressing industrial concerns in Mexico at this time. "Mexican industry," President López Portillo has affirmed, "was organized on the basis of import substitution, which dominated a market that is now saturated. It now does not generate enough employment and has shown its incapacity to produce goods that satisfy the needs of the mass of people." [34]

Tourism

Mexican government spokesmen have gone on record suggesting that 3 million Mexicans earn their living directly or indirectly from tourism. [35] "Tourism," one government advertisement in a United States publication recently explained, "is Mexico's biggest business." [36]

---

[33] *Ibid.*

[34] "The Next President of Mexico Views the Issues," *Business Week*, August 9, 1976, p. 50.

[35] "Today, 3,000,000 Mexicans earn their living from tourism," advertisement of the Mexican government, *New York Times*, September 8, 1976, p. C-55.

[36] "Mexico—The Echeverría Years," p. 22.

Since 1960, tourism has grown nearly fivefold so that it is, in fact, a major source of revenue and employment in modern-day Mexico. In 1974, for example, more than 83 million tourists— 95 percent of them American citizens—took vacations in the country or visited Mexican border towns. By mid-1974, Mexican tourist authorities estimated that "it would be necessary to train a minimum of 70,000 additional personnel [to be] concerned directly with tourism in the next five years." [37] By 1977, about 400,000 Mexicans were directly employed in tourism activities. But in addition to the added employment opportunities that it generates, tourism also brings the country a significant capital inflow. During the first eight months of 1975 alone, Mexico's gross earnings from tourism totaled US$1.66 billion. This income, however, represented a low 2.6 percent gain over the earnings from tourism registered during the same period in 1974. It was a significant drop from the annual 12 percent growth rate that had previously been the norm. Excluding border traffic earnings, Mexico's 1976 foreign exchange revenues from tourism amounted to only US$820 million.[38]

Several factors explain the successes and shortcomings of Mexico's tourism infrastructure and its ability to create new jobs and attract foreign currency revenues. One factor is a series of federal moves that have made tourism a priority industry in Mexico and reflect the government's mobilization to attract more tourists. For instance, a Tourism Secretariat was recently created, the director of which is a member of the presidential cabinet. The country's 1974 Tourism Development Law also made tourism a priority concern by calling for the development of new tourist sites and jobs and by creating a National Tourism Development Fund (*Fondo Nacional de Turismo*—FONATUR) for the development of both. In May 1977, Mexico secured a US$42 million loan from the World Bank specifically to develop tourist sites in Baja California and thereby create jobs for some 12,000 people directly and some 13,000 others in handicrafts, food processing, and transportation. These innovations, Mexican officials have pointed out, are aimed at increasing tourism's contribution to Mexico's BOP (Balance of Payments).[39]

---

[37] Weil *et al.*, *Area Handbook*, p. 43.

[38] "Mexico—The Echeverría Years," p. 22; The World Bank, "World Bank Lends $42 million to Mexico for Tourism," Bank News Release No. 77/101, Washington, D.C., May 12, 1977.

[39] Echeverría Álvarez, *Quinto Informe de Gobierno*, p. 42.

Mexico's sophisticated network of roads and highways facilitate the visits of American and Canadian tourists by car. Today, Mexico boasts 10,000 trailer parking spaces, 6,700 hotels with 190,000 rooms, and 10,000 restaurants and bars. The country's comparatively lower food and lodging prices have also played a key role in stimulating a heavy tourist trade.

Since 1974, however, Mexico's tourism industry has suffered several setbacks. Notably, the growth rate of tourism in the country has tapered off as the result of three developments: (1) the impact of the United States recession on American travel abroad, (2) the Jewish boycott on travel to Mexico, and (3) the escalation of local food and lodging prices.

"If the U.S. sneezes," one popular expression in Mexico goes, "Mexico catches the cold." The fact is that Mexico's economic performance is intimately tied to United States economic trends. We shall review this phenomenon in more detail in subsequent sections on trade and economic growth. It suffices to point out here that a tight economic climate in the United States tends to restrict critically United States tourism in Mexico, thereby cutting back important revenues and job opportunities on the Mexican side of the border. As Mexican sources themselves have affirmed, "The slower pace of [tourism] growth in 1975 is seen as an effect of the U.S. recession." [40]

Second, Mexico's anti-Zionist vote in the United Nations in November 1975 resulted in a Jewish tourist boycott that has also had a critical impact on tourism incomes. According to one report:

> The issue that caused most uproar was Mexico's support [under President Echeverría] for the . . . U.N. resolution equating Zionism with racism. Most observers felt this position reflected Mexico's anxiety to prove its Third World credentials, rather than any upsurge of anti-Semitism. Nevertheless, several large American-Jewish organizations called a tourist boycott of Mexico which almost immediately resulted in the cancellation of thousands of hotel rooms and several large conventions, and served as a sharp reminder of Mexico's extreme vulnerability to economic pressures from the U.S.[41]

Third, Mexican food and lodging prices have sharply escalated in recent years, taking away some of the practical inducement

---

[40] "Mexico—The Echeverría Years," p. 22.

[41] Alan Riding, "Mexican Foreign Policy—A Bit Too Independent," *Financial Times*, January 8, 1976, p. 4.

of the country's previously low cost of travel. In an effort to restrain inflation, for example, government officials recently imposed a 15 percent tax on the meals served in all class-A restaurants throughout Mexico. Continuous wage increases have also had a negative impact. Indeed, Mexico is in the grip of a wage-price spiral: wage increases provoke consumer price hikes which, in turn, add fuel to labor demands for higher wages. In the tourism industry, the effect of this spiral is felt in greater service, maintenance, and construction costs, and, ultimately, in hotel and restaurant bills which increase steeply each year and which may prompt foreign tourists to reconsider the prospect of a visit to Mexico. Thus, Mexico's tourism business, a United States study relates, "declined 4% in 1975, owing largely to price increases that had made once cheap Mexico City as costly for Americans as many European cities." [42]

At the present time, of course, Mexico still ranks among the world's less expensive tourist centers because of the country's recent devaluations. A change in United States tax laws, however, now eliminates tax deductions for United States business conventions held abroad under most conditions. This development may offset a considerable amount of the exchange-rate incentive for Mexican travel. Furthermore, the prospect of continued inflation and higher prices is an ominous threat to the growth of Mexico's tourist trade, a threat which the Mexican government must counter.

THE ROLE OF STATE AND FOREIGN INVESTMENTS IN THE MEXICAN ECONOMY

Mexico's is a "mixed economy," combining foreign, private domestic, and government investments. Each makes significant contributions to specific sectors of the Mexican economy. As one survey of the equity concentrations of Mexico's businesses has pointed out:

> The economy of Mexico can best be described as a mixed economy with the government, its agencies or government-owned or controlled companies dominant in the areas of public utilities and certain basic manufacturing industries. . . . Private enterprise is the principal factor in manufacturing, banking and finance, commerce, . . . and the services industries, although large government-owned companies

---

[42] "Down Goes the Peso," *Time*, September 13, 1976, p. 50.

now exist in all these areas. . . . Foreign investment is most frequently found in manufacturing and mining, and with less frequency in other areas.[43]

It is significant, however, that private domestic investment has been on the decline in the last decade while government participation in the economy has expanded. Mexico's president has sometimes expressed a dim view of the private sector, suggesting that ' "private initiative extremists would like . . . no raises for workers nor better prices for peasants; that is that the whole system work to make them even richer, and in no way can we permit this." ' [44] Not surprisingly, the current administration's avowed development policy calls for "coordinated" public and private investments in the economy under a new federal program, the Popular Production Alliance, so as to "try to boost private production, but not at the expense of government participation in the economy." [45] ' "If private enterprise does not invest," ' López Portillo has stated, ' "the public sector must." ' [46]

The facts are that Mexico's economy is already highly centralized, and that there are currently more than 700 state-owned enterprises in virtually every field of Mexican economic activity. As mentioned previously, the government is the principal owner of Mexico's largest steel companies, the telephone company, the largest producers of sulphur, and the national petroleum monopoly. In addition to these, there are principal government investments in copper refining, commercial banks, water supply and irrigation, investment banks, electric utilities, supermarket chains, sugar mills, and a host of other activities. In 1976, in fact, Mexican officials announced that government participation in the economy represented 45 percent of the national product.[47]

Thus, the government has an extensive investment presence in Mexico and is the country's major employer. Furthermore, state intervention in the economy is escalating sharply. Since 1970 at least, the number of state-owned corporations in Mexico jumped

---

[43] Price Waterhouse & Co., *Doing Business in Mexico*, p. 16.

[44] William Giandoni, "Mexicans Suffer Crisis of Confidence," *Times of the Americas*, March 31, 1976, p. 5.

[45] "Mexico—The Echeverría Years," p. 42.

[46] "The Next President of Mexico Views the Issues," p. 50.

[47] "Mexico—The Echeverría Years," p. 20.

from 86 to 740.[48] Analysts of Mexico's economic development additionally note:

> In 1975, it was estimated that state-owned firms contributed 47% of the federal budget, and the figure is rising. The state has also intervened strongly to force "import substitution"—to replace imported products by their Mexican-produced equivalents—as well as "Mexicanization," to give either the government or private Mexican interests a controlling share of foreign-owned firms. The government sets export quotas for industry; . . . controls the prices of key consumer goods, such as food, and through the labor wing of the PRI controls the wages paid to workers.[49]

Effective February 1976, a new mining law increased "to a considerable extent the intervention of the government in the operation and control of private investment in the mining industry."[50] Moreover, in October 1976, the president of Volkswagen's Mexican subsidiary, Hans Barschkis, announced that his firm had begun negotiations with government officials on the possibility of a Volkswagen de México merger with the Mexican government. Volkswagen's 1975 sales in Mexico had reportedly dropped 15 percent below their 1974 level, and the company registered heavy losses in 1976 with the devaluation of the peso. According to informed sources at the time of Barschkis' announcement, however:

> The negotiations received hefty impetus from . . . [a] Presidential recommendation of a 16% to 21% wage boost for all organized workers in Mexico. VW de Mexico will have to pay the new raises on top of a 20% pay boost that its 7,000 employees won in July after an eight-day strike. . . . The hope is that if the government becomes a partner, it will speed up [auto] price boosts.[51]

The merger did not occur. Volkswagen, however, won the right to lay off 3,000 of its 10,000 employees that it was previously forced to maintain on its payroll despite the sharp sales decline.[52]

---

[48] Richard A. Shaffer, "Mexico: More Trouble Ahead?," *Wall Street Journal*, November 23, 1976, p. 24.

[49] John Godfrey, "How Long Can Delicate Balance Be Maintained?," *Financial Post*, July 7, 1976, p. 7.

[50] Price Waterhouse & Co., *Mexico*, supplement to *Doing Business in Mexico* (New York: Price Waterhouse & Co., 1976), p. 2.

[51] "Mexico—VW Talks Merger with the Government," *Business Week*, October 11, 1976, p. 48. See also "Volkswagen Denial on Mexico," *Financial Times*, May 13, 1977, p. 33.

[52] "Volkswagen Mexiko in Finanzkrise geraten," *Süddeutsche Zeitung*, November 8, 1976; and "Volkswagen. Erst mal warten," *Der Spiegel*, No. 45, November 1, 1976, p. 2.

The preeminence of the state in Mexico's economy has gone beyond the point of facilitating rapid economic growth and macroeconomic efficiency on three counts. First, extensive state intervention in the economy puts the government in the delicate position of being both Mexico's major employer and labor's close political ally. Wage adjustments have become an embroiled political and economic tug-of-war as a result. If firms such as Volkswagen see government mergers as a means of offsetting rising labor costs or lowering price ceilings, organized labor in Mexico envisions them as a means of gaining better wage increases and tighter price controls in an economy more centralized under the PRI.

Second, Mexico's economic problems and recent devaluations make tight control of the country's federal deficit—and, therefore, fewer federal outlays for state-owned firms—genuinely imperative. At the present time, state-owned corporations absorb more than one-half of the government's total expenditures. This spending has increased considerably since 1973 "to cover the increases in prices of consumers' goods and for salaries of public sector employees." [53]

Third, large-scale government intervention in the economy has helped nurture extensive corruption in many Mexican businesses, a fact which again tends to weaken the public's support of PRI rule. According to one report:

> . . . Large-scale corruption is at the higher levels of government —particularly in the state-owned decentralized agencies, such as the oil monopoly Pemex, the federal electricity commissions and the Altos Hornos Steel Company. At these levels "commissions" or kickbacks of between 5 and 10 percent on contracts are considered normal.
>
> "Of course, nothing as sordid as money changes hands," said one lawyer who has experience in negotiating such commissions on behalf of clients. "The commission is built into the contract price and is usually paid into a numbered account in Switzerland or the Bahamas. The companies don't mind because the commission comes out of public funds rather than company profits." [54]

Direct foreign investment is welcomed and encouraged in Mexico, but it represents only 5 percent of total public and pri-

---

[53] Inter-American Development Bank, *Economic and Social Progress*, p. 344; Shaffer, "Mexico: More Troubles Ahead?," p. 24.

[54] Alan Riding, "Corruption Again Election Issue in Mexico," *New York Times*, June 29, 1976, p. 2.

vate investment.[55] Indeed, Mexico's government officials are eager to attract foreign private investments which bring new technology into the country, accelerate exports, or create new jobs. "Foreign investment," López Portillo has affirmed, "is welcome and necessary. It signifies access to markets we do not have, technology we do not have, and financing that is useful to us. *But we want partners, not bosses.*" [56] That qualification, we shall see, is an important one.

Hundreds of United States, European, and Japanese-based multinationals currently have major equity holdings in Mexico, and United States Department of Commerce data show that United States corporate investments in the country climbed from just over $2 billion in mid-1973 to $3.2 billion at year-end 1975.[57] According to Al R. Wichtrich, president of AmCham Mexico, a survey carried out by the Stanford Research Institute among companies representing 41 percent of the American investments in Mexico showed that an average 76.2 percent of the 1975 profits of these firms were reinvested in the Mexican economy.[58] Eighty-five percent of the United States firms with Mexican affiliates polled, the Institute reported, had "no regrets about investing in Mexico." [59] (See Table III-5.)

Several facts regarding the confidence of foreign investors in Mexico and government attempts there to take on "partners, not bosses" must, however, be made clear. First, the Stanford Research Institute survey was undertaken prior to Mexico's devaluations of the peso in August and October 1976 at a time when Mexico's currency maintained its long-time fixed parity to the United States dollar. For United States investors in Mexico, there was no exposure risk in Mexico at that time. But Mexico's two devaluations in 1976 and conversion to a floating exchange rate have since had a "considerable depressing effect on the profits of many U.S. concerns with Mexican affiliates." [60] Indeed,

---

[55] Price Waterhouse & Co., *Doing Business in Mexico*, p. 17.

[56] "The Next President of Mexico Views the Issues," p. 50. (Italics added.)

[57] Richard A. Shaffer, "Multinationals Discover Profits in Mexico Despite Peso Problems, Ownership Rules," *Wall Street Journal*, November 5, 1976, p. 36.

[58] "Mexico—A Free and Democratic Society," advertisement of the American Chamber of Commerce of Mexico, *Wall Street Journal*, September 1, 1976, p. 9.

[59] Shaffer, "Multinationals Discover Profits," p. 36.

[60] *Ibid.*

TABLE III-5

U.S. Direct Foreign Investments in Mexico and Rates of Return, 1974 and 1975

(Millions of US dollars)

Year	Investments							Total Increase in Investments since 1970:	
	Manu-facturing	Percent Rate of Return	Petroleum $	Percent Rate of Return	Total $	Percent Rate of Return		$	% Increase
1975	2,433	14.3	21	33.3	3,177	14.1		1,391	77.9
1974	2,173	13.4	18	44.4	2,854	13.8		—	—

Source: "U.S. Total Direct Foreign Investment and Rate of Return, 1970-1975," *Business International*, January 14, 1977, pp. 14-15.

Note: Direct Foreign Investment Total ($ figures) represents the value of U.S. parents' net equity in and loans to foreign affiliates. Rate of Return (% figures) represents adjusted earnings of these affiliates divided by direct investment. Adjusted earnings consist of U.S. parents' share in their affiliates' earnings, less foreign withholding taxes on dividends paid by affiliates to parents, plus interest received from affiliates on intercompany accounts.

this explains the recent plight of Volkswagen's financial performance in Mexico and that of many other multinational firms as well.

Second, joint ventures are virtually mandatory in Mexico with very few exceptions. A new law for the Promotion of Mexican Investment and Regulation of Foreign Investment, effective May 1973, requires foreigners to join with 51 percent local shareholders. Although not retroactive, "the essence of the law," government sources point out, "is that foreign ownership of new investments is limited to 49%, is restricted to 40% in industries deemed vital (such as petrochemicals), and is ruled out in certain businesses (oil exploration and production are reserved for the Mexican government)." [61] Companies formed prior to the law but not controlled by a majority of Mexican nationals are preempted from many tax and other incentives. For example, "Mexicanized" firms—those which are 51 percent or more owned by Mexicans—pay only 50 percent of the federal portion (usually over 90 percent) of both Mexico's production and general export taxes.[62] Moreover, the acquisition by foreigners of more than 49 percent of the fixed assets or 25 percent of the capital stock of a Mexican company requires the prior authorization of a new federal agency, the National Commission on Foreign Investment. The rulings of this body tend to be flexible, but a recent survey of the Commission's decisions from 1973 through mid-1975 shows that only six of fourteen requests to organize companies with more than 49 percent foreign ownership and twenty out of thirty-six petitions of existing companies controlled by foreigners for authorization to enter new product lines or economic activities were given approval.[63] As a result, one late 1976 report relates that:

> In recent years, hundreds of . . . U.S. subsidiaries have teamed up with Mexican investors to skirt the roadblocks to growth thrown up by the government. Some of these U.S. investments are souring, particularly as a result of two effective devaluations of the peso . . . that have put the currency's dollar value more than 50% under its level before August 31. But many other companies seem likely to weather this crisis, including the affiliates of Phillips Petroleum Co., Dana Corp., RCA Corp., Robert Bosch of West Germany and SKF of Sweden, all of which are part of the DESC group [*Desar-*

---

[61] Director General de Informacion, "Mexico, Today and Tomorrow," p. 9.

[62] Price Waterhouse & Co., *Doing Business in Mexico*, p. 94.

[63] *Ibid.*, p. 25.

rollo Economico Sociedad Civil, one of several professional Mexican holding companies which form partnerships with foreign interests but leave day-to-day operations in the hands of partner managers].[64]

Interestingly enough, joint ventures with Mexican holding companies such as DESC are sometimes helpful in defusing labor problems as well as in simplifying compliance with Mexico's ownership rules. In 1975, for example, a union strike paralyzed the operations of Dana Corporation's Spicer subsidiary in Mexico of which DESC is an equity partner. DESC and Spicer officers both negotiated with Mexican Ministry of Labor officials until the government agreed to order the strikers back to work. ' "We would have been dead without them," ' Dana's President Gerald Mitchell later remarked. ' "They [DESC] took a very hard line which, as foreigners, we could never have gotten away with." ' [65]

Another point worthy of note is that foreign technology agreements in Mexico have come under very close scrutiny in recent years. Mexico's 1973 Law on the Transfer of Technology created yet another federal agency, the Technology Transfer Registry, which must approve technology agreements between foreign companies and their local affiliate licensees. As one report notes:

> The agency rejects contracts that require "excessive" payments for technology or that restrict its use. . . .
> In the past two years, the Mexican registry has reviewed and approved 4,500 existing technology contracts—with considerable changes in some cases. Fees collected by foreign pharmaceutical companies from their Mexican subsidiaries and licensees, for example, have been knocked down from an average 5% on sales to 2% for most companies.[66]

Finally, it should be pointed out that foreign investment interest has cooled off considerably in Mexico due to the country's floating exchange rate and mounting labor costs. The heavy toll of Mexico's 1976 devaluations on multinational profit remittances has already been described. ' "With the effective devaluation," ' one Mexican stock broker stated flatly, ' "a foreign company loses on the currency exchange rate if it wants to repatriate capital." ' [67] Rising labor costs—as the Volkswagen example might

---

[64] Shaffer, "Multinationals Discover Profits," p. 36.

[65] *Ibid.*

[66] "Latin America Opens the Door to Foreign Investment Again," p. 46.

[67] "Winners and Losers as the Peso Floats," *Business Week,* September 20, 1976, p. 36.

suggest—are also beginning to sour investment interest. This is especially true since the government announced its controversial 1977 tax law, which enjoins firms to employ *more* workers and newer technology or pay tax on any profits considered in excess of a normal profits-to-income ratio. The result, according to *Business Latin America*, is that

> . . . Foreign investment is folding: from $362 million in 1975 to $330 million in 1976. If the system holds steady this year [1977], foreign investment should pick up in 1978, but few companies are in a hurry to invest and some are selling out. Cyanamid sold its Cyanaquim Mexican subsidiary to the Mexican chemical group CYDSA early this year, and Philco sold its entire operation to the Monterrey holding company Alfa last year.[68]

MEXICAN ECONOMIC GROWTH

Mexico's economy has registered accelerated rates of growth in past years, and Latin American publications have proudly ranked the country's growth record in the 1960s among the world's highest indexes.[69] Even in late 1976, official Mexican government sources insisted that

> Businessmen appreciate Mexico's investment climate, and see Mexico's past growth as a healthy portend [*sic*] of future prosperity.
> Take, for instance, gross domestic product (gross national product less earnings on foreign investments). Since 1940, Mexico's G.D.P. has averaged [a growth rate of] 7.2%. This exceeds the growth of the U.S. (4.6%), West Germany (4.6%), or any other Latin nation including Brazil (4.8%).[70]

A closer look at Mexico's economic performance in recent years, however, is anything but encouraging. The country's 1971-1975 average growth index dropped several points below the 7.2 percent rate touted by the government to a more moderate 5.6 percent.[71] Specifically, Mexico's gross domestic product increased by 3.4 percent, 7.3 percent, and 7.6 percent, respec-

---

[68] "Business Outlook—Mexico," *Business Latin America*, March 9, 1977, p. 77.

[69] A review of Mexico's economic growth since the 1960s is provided in *Imagem do Brasil e da America Latina*, p. 59.

[70] Director General de Informacion, "Mexico, Today and Tomorrow," p. 9.

[71] "Latin America Opens the Door to Foreign Investment Again," p. 33.

TABLE III-6
Real Annual Growth Rates by Sector
(Percentages)

Sector	1950-60	1962	1964	1966	1968	1970	1974	1975
Agriculture	4.4	6.8	10.3	1.5	1.6	5.5	-0.7	4.0 [a]
Livestock	4.4	-1.5	3.1	2.2	6.7	5.7	3.4	—
Forestry	-0.3	2.6	[c]	-0.7	2.3	2.9	2.0	2.0
Fishing	5.9	-2.9	-2.4	11.2	-11.0	12.4	1.7	-8.0
Mining	2.8	8.9	2.2	2.8	2.2	1.5	13.4	9.5
Petroleum [b]	7.6	5.3	9.0	5.0	8.6	9.9	16.2	12.0
Petrochemicals	n.a.	110.5	41.8	23.3	33.6	7.6	17.4	4.0
Manufacturing	7.3	4.6	17.4	9.4	10.1	9.2	5.4	3.5
Construction	7.2	6.5	16.9	14.4	7.4	4.6	3.8	7.5
Electrical Energy	9.2	8.9	16.5	14.0	19.7	11.0	10.1	—
Communications and Transportation	6.2	4.6	7.1	8.3	10.8	7.9	11.4	7.0
Commerce	5.9	3.4	13.4	7.4	8.5	8.5	6.0	—
Government	4.4	12.8	10.4	7.7	9.6	5.3	8.2	10.0
Other Services	7.4	3.9	5.7	4.4	6.5	6.5	3.7	—
Gross Domestic Product	6.1 [d]	4.7	11.7	6.9	8.1	7.7	5.9	3.8-4.2

Sources: Ronald A. Krieger, *Mexico: An Economic Survey* (New York: First National City Bank, 1971), p. 13; and *Mexico*, Economist Intelligence Unit Quarterly Economic Review No. 2 (London: EIU, 1976), p. 4.

[a] Estimate.
[b] 1950-1970 figures include coal production data.
[c] Less than 0.1.
[d] GNP.
n.a. Not available.

tively, in 1971, 1972, and 1973.[72] In 1975, this economic growth measure fell from the previous year's 5.9 percent level to the low 3.8-4.2 percent range, a level "barely ahead of . . . [the country's] booming population growth rate of 3.6%."[73] Clearly, an economic slowdown was already in effect.

Another fact is that federal outlays in Mexico's economy have come to play a key role in fanning GDP growth. According to an Inter-American Bank report, in fact, the main factor behind Mexico's excellent 1973 growth record (7.6 percent) was "the increase in total investment—up 27.4 percent over 1972—and especially public investment, which rose 57.5 percent and represented half of the total."[74] The critical implication, then, is that the growth of Mexico's very centralized economy is closely related to the volume of federal investments in it. But as the recent decision to postpone additional federal expenditures in the Las Truchas steel project makes clear, federal spending is being slowed down. Indeed, Mexico's current administration is committed to cutting back federal spending in an attempt to curb inflation and improve the country's credit-worthiness. This commitment became imperative in 1976 when Mexico's extensive foreign debt, pressing debt-servicing obligations, two effective devaluations of the peso, and very high rate of inflation prompted the International Monetary Fund and the international banking community to "suggest" austerity measures. New projects such as Las Truchas have therefore been postponed, the payment of many public sector domestic debts has been delayed, and even the wages of some federal bureaucrats are being paid late.

The result is that Mexico's economic development has lost considerable speed. One analyst succinctly observed, "Efforts to prevent inflation caused by excessive Government spending, perhaps the main fuel for inflation during the Echeverría administration, have so far been . . . successful, although at the cost of minimum economic activity."[75] Mexico's gross domestic product grew by a mere 2 percent in 1976, the country's worst record since 1953. What is more, economic growth is expected to fall to the all-time

---

[72] Inter-American Development Bank, *Economic and Social Progress*, p. 343.

[73] "Latin America Opens the Door to Foreign Investment Again," p. 38.

[74] Inter-American Development Bank, *Economic and Social Progress*, p. 343.

[75] Alan Riding, "Mexico's Inflation Fight: Stomach vs. Program," *New York Times*, April 16, 1977, p. 33.

low of "1% or even less" in 1977, according to respected forecasts.[76] (See Figure III-2.)

Thus, recent Mexican growth trends make abundantly clear
that all is not well in Mexico's economy. The government has
had to sacrifice economic growth for greater financial discipline.
This policy has implications which are alarming and critical. On
the one hand, merely to maintain current standards of living in
the country, Mexico's minimum real growth rate must necessarily
exceed 3.6 percent to match the country's population boom. If it
does not, Mexico's *per capita* indexes and living standards will
fall, jeopardizing labor's support of the PRI and the country's
renowned political stability. On the other hand, certain economic problems in Mexico beg government correction—even at
the possible expense of labor's dissatisfaction. As one British
report on Mexico's dilemma has noted:

> There is a consensus that a period of economic austerity is un-
> avoidable to stabilise the peso, to control inflation and to meet the
> conditions for further credit imposed by the International Monetary
> Fund and the foreign banking community. But it is still not clear
> which sectors . . . will pay the main price for this austerity, al-
> though greater unemployment, lower wage increases and tighter
> credit seem likely.[77]

MEXICAN TRADE AND THE BALANCE OF PAYMENTS

Mexico is one of the world's major trading nations and officials in
Mexico City are quick to extol the country's fast trade growth.
Between 1970 and late 1976, government spokesmen point out,
Mexican exports to the United States more than doubled, while
United States exports to Mexico tripled in sales volume during
the same period.[78] Nevertheless, these facts underscore two damaging weaknesses of Mexico's foreign trade as well as its impressive expansion strength. First, Mexican trade continues to evidence heavy dependence on the United States, which has been
historically Mexico's dominant trading partner. Second, foreign
trade balances typically register large deficits in Mexico and
have a heavy negative impact on the country's balance of
payments.

---

[76] "Mexico: The Next Five Years," *Business International*, March 18, 1977,
p. 85.

[77] Alan Riding, "Mending the Broken Bridges," *Financial Times*, November 30, 1976, p. 7.

[78] Director General de Informacion, "Mexico, Today and Tomorrow," p. 9.

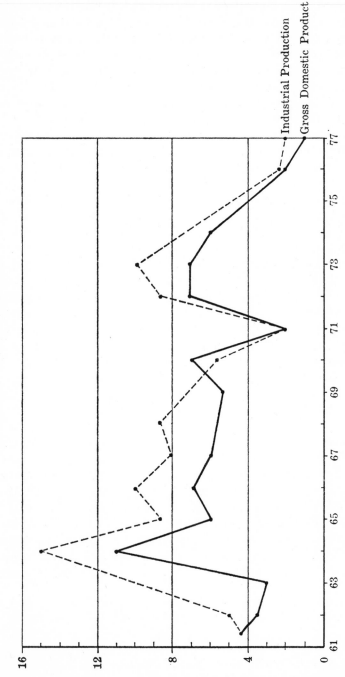

FIGURE III-2
Mexican Economic Growth Trends

Industrial Production

Gross Domestic Product

Source: Reprinted from page 84 of the March 18, 1977 issue of *Business International* with the permission of the publisher, Business International Corporation (New York).

Although the United States' economic cycles have somewhat diminished in importance as a source of instability in Mexico's economy, commerce between the two countries is still one of the most vital factors of Mexico's economic growth. The historically close correlation of Mexican trade to the United States' economic performance is presented in Table III-7. Even today, "a modest change in the structure of supply and demand in either country can . . . have a major influence on Mexican trade flows." [79] That is to say, a recession in the United States can potentially cripple Mexico's export revenues. The dangerous implication, to reiterate Mexico's own popular expression, is that "if the U.S. sneezes, Mexico catches the cold."

Since the early 1970s, Mexico's government officials have made a concerted effort to diversify the country's trade flows, attempting to step up trade with Japan, Europe, and other Latin republics. This mobilization has met with only partial success. Mexican trade with countries other than the United States has certainly increased, but the dominance of the United States as Mexico's chief trading partner has lessened only slightly. In 1974, Mexican exports bound for the United States represented 62.2 percent of Mexico's total export sales; in 1975, this proportion may have actually *increased* by several percentage points according to the initial tabulations of respected studies.[80]

A second important characteristic of Mexico's foreign trade is that Mexican imports typically exceed exports (see Table III-8). Statistics on Mexican trade differ widely from one source to the next so that Mexico's yearly trade imbalances are somewhat hard to pinpoint. By all accounts, however, Mexico has suffered continuous and growing trade deficits over the last eight years. For example, the country's trade deficit with the United States reportedly grew from some $527 million in 1971 to $2.48 billion in 1975 despite sizeable United States purchases of Mexican oil.[81] This trade record has consistently drained Mexico's exchange reserves and resulted in negative current account balances. It has, according to local businessmen, forced the Mexican government to encourage tourism and increase net foreign bor-

---

[79] Clark W. Reynolds, *The Mexican Economy: Twentieth Century Structure and Growth* (New Haven: Yale University Press, 1970), p. 199.

[80] Percentage computed from data in Table III-8, p. 47.

[81] Alan Riding, "Mexico Begins Export Offensive with Biggest Fair in San Antonio," *New York Times*, September 9, 1976, p. C-58.

TABLE III-7

The Relationship Between U.S. Industrial Production,
Mexican Exports, and Mexican Industrial Production
(coefficients of correlation)

Period	Quarters Lagged [a]	Mexican Commodity Exports Correlated with U.S. Industrial Production	Mexican Industrial Production Correlated with Mexican Commodity Exports
	—2	0.81	0.26
1937	—1	0.42	0.21
to	0	0.18	0.45
1940	+1	0.07	0.42
	+2	0.04	0.62
	—2	0.57	0.75
1941	—1	0.62	0.76
to	0	0.82	0.80
1945	+1	0.52	0.77
	+2	0.48	0.72
	—2	0.35	0.64
1946	—1	0.69	0.50
to	0	0.82	0.06
1950	+1	0.79	0.48
	+2	0.48	0.72
	—2	0.32	0.20
1951	—1	0.26	0.42
to	0	0.18	0.40
1955	+1	0.33	0.01
	+2	0.23	0.50
	—2	0.01	0.47
1956	—1	0.10	0.41
to	0	0.83	0.46
1960	+1	0.72	0.30
	+2	0.68	0.37

Source: Clark W. Reynolds, *The Mexican Economy—Twentieth Century
Structure and Growth* (New Haven and London: Yale University
Press, 1970), p. 244, quoting Luis Antonio Aspra Rodriguez, "La
transmisión de las fluctuaciones cíclicas a la economía Mexicana"
(thesis, Universidad Nacional Autónoma de México, 1964), Table 10.
[a] The figures in this column have a negative sign when the dependent
variable follows the independent variable and vice versa.

TABLE III-8
Mexican Foreign Trade
(Millions of US Dollars)

	1970	1971	1972	1973	1974
Exports Worldwide	1205.4	1320.5	1844.6	2631.5	2850.0
U.S.	846.8	917.9	1297.0	1810.9	1524.0
Japan	68.9	65.3	118.2	177.8	120.3
West Germany	27.8	33.9	39.3	59.7	108.8
Brazil	14.7	25.8	34.0	43.2	83.2
Venezuela	21.9	24.6	38.8	38.0	40.7
Imports Worldwide	2460.7	2407.2	2935.0	4145.6	6056.7
U.S.	1567.5	1479.1	1774.4	2609.4	3778.7
West Germany	185.1	205.2	263.6	278.5	476.4
Japan	86.0	89.9	115.4	177.9	223.6
France	104.6	75.7	83.6	100.2	131.9
United Kingdom	71.6	67.5	92.9	90.6	136.0
Principal Exports Worldwide					
Cotton	82.7	63.4	148.7	166.5	—
Vegetables (Fresh, Frozen, and Preserved)	52.3	49.5	137.4	179.0	—
Sugar and Honey	102.9	107.3	125.7	141.0	—
Live Domestic Animals	30.9	24.0	116.8	91.3	—
Coffee	74.5	73.2	95.1	168.7	—
Principal Imports Worldwide					
Road Motor Vehicles	249.1	268.3	293.1	376.4	—
Misc. Nonelectrical Machinery and Appliances	226.8	210.6	243.8	308.0	—
Organic Chemicals	113.6	134.1	165.4	196.2	—
Misc. Electrical Machinery	104.7	86.6	125.8	171.5	—
Textile, Leather Machinery	72.8	88.6	120.1	96.6	—

Source: United Nations, Department of Economic and Social Affairs, *Yearbook of International Statistics, 1975,* Vol. 1 (New York: United Nations, 1976), pp. 665-669.

rowing to close the trade gap.[82] This fact, coupled with Mexico's earlier borrowing penchant to finance the country's development projects, has made Mexican public and foreign debt soar. By year-end 1976, Mexico's long-term overseas debt had surpassed $20 billion, and the burden of servicing it became a substantially large number in Mexico's balance of payments.[83]

To correct the country's deficits, Mexico's government has stepped up its aggressive trade improvement campaign which hinges on import substitution, a host of export incentives, and, most recently, a more favorable peso exchange rate. Import substitution has long been an espoused federal priority. Since World War II, it has been implemented through strict import licensing controls, steep protective tariffs, and "government purchasing policies, trade and payments and compensation agreements." [84] The subtle implication here is that government officials are indeed mindful of the negative impact that rising labor costs can have on the competitiveness of Mexican products and the success of the country's drives for import substitution and export growth. But as Mexico's trade record and local businessmen can attest, the need to keep labor costs in tow for export gains has sometimes been overlooked in the PRI's effort to keep peace with labor.

Enforced industrialization is another strategy that has been used for many years to curb imports and improve the country's trade flows:

> Enforced industrialization . . . was initiated in 1962 when the Government decreed that fixed amounts of Mexican-made components must be included in typewriters and automotive vehicles manufactured in Mexico, within specified periods of time. Since then, similar decrees have required the manufacture of agricultural tractors, certain kinds of construction machinery, diesel engines, and other products . . . assembled in Mexico largely from imported parts.[85]

In July, August, and December of 1975, however, Mexico's government promulgated a series of laws aimed at curbing imports

---

[82] Notes from author's conversations with Mexican businessmen and entrepreneurs, April 15, 1977, Philadelphia, PA.

[83] *Mexico*, Economist Intelligence Unit QER No. 3 (London: EIU, 1976), p. 7.

[84] U.S. Department of Commerce, *Establishing a Business in Mexico*, OBR72-027 (Washington, D.C.: U.S. Government Printing Office, 1972), p. 4.

[85] *Ibid.*

FIGURE III-3
Foreign Trade Trends in Mexico

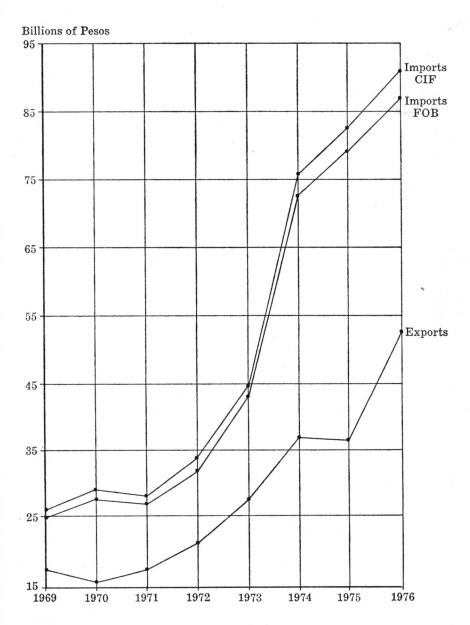

Billions of Pesos

Imports CIF

Imports FOB

Exports

Source: International Monetary Fund, "Mexico," *International Financial Statistics*, Vol. XXX, No. 5 (May 1977), p. 279.

Mexico

Table III-9
Mexico's Balance of Payments
(US$ Millions)

	1973	1974	1975
Exports of goods	2,071	2,850	2,859
Production of gold & silver	70	149	140
Tourism	724	842	801
Border trade	1,208	1,373	1,519
Assembly plant operations	278	443	446
Other	477	685	538
Total exports of goods & services	4,828	6,342	6,303
Imports of goods	3,813	6,057	6,580
Tourism	258	335	398
Border trade	695	819	934
Remittances on investment	528	634	699
Interest on official debts	379	588	779
Other	331	468	557
Total imports of goods & services	6,004	8,901	9,947
Current account balance	—1,175	—2,558	—3,643
Errors & omissions & short-term capital movements	—378	—136	—82
Capital account:			
direct foreign investment	287	362	362
operations with securities	—10	—60	137
new foreign credits	1,371	1,999	2,952
loans abroad	—19	—40	5
net government debt	70	471	460
other	—22	—2	—26
total	1,076	2,731	3,890
Overall balance of payments	122	37	165

Source: *Mexico*, Economist Intelligence Unit Quarterly Economic Report No. 3 (London: EIU, 1976), pp. 6 and 7.

with even greater vigor. Import duties were increased on some 3,000 tariff items, and the number of items classified as luxury goods (*ad valorem* duties of 50 to 100 percent) jumped from 652 to 1,320.[86] At the same time, taxes on many export items were abolished, and tax rebate incentives for exporters were enhanced. Firms exporting products which have a national content of 40 percent or more now receive higher refunds (Table III-10) on the taxes paid on the production and sale of export articles and the materials used to produce them.

An aggressive export marketing campaign has also been launched under the Mexican Foreign Trade Institute (*Instituto Mexicano de Comercio Exterior*—IMCE). From 1970 through 1976, this government agency sponsored ninety-five trade fairs, forty-seven trade missions, and the trips of 105 special trade envoys around the world.[87] Of course, Mexico's devaluations of the peso in 1976 lent some muscle to the export offensive as well. As former President Echeverría stated at the opening of Mexico's largest trade fair in Texas only a week after the peso was effectively devalued some 40 percent, ' "The reactivation of the United States economy has opened new trade opportunities for Mexico . . . which is why we are exhibiting our . . . products at a time when the monetary adjustments we have made make the prices of our articles more attractive." ' [88]

These kinds of trade improvement efforts in Mexico are now beginning to show some positive results. According to a 1977 *Business Latin America* survey:

> In this respect, the peso float is working. Imports fell by $550 million last year (8.4%), while exports went up $439 million (15.4%), meaning the trade deficit narrowed by $1 billion from $3.7 billion to $2.7 billion. Imports are dropping, mainly in consumer goods and production materials columns, but increasing in capital goods and equipment.[89]

Three facts suggest, however, that greater revisions of Mexico's trade flows will not be achieved until massive oil exports bring

---

[86] Price Waterhouse & Co., *Mexico*, p. 2.

[87] "Mexico—The Echeverría Years," p. 37.

[88] Riding, "Mexico Begins Export Offensive with Biggest Fair in San Antonio," p. C-58.

[89] "Business Outlook—Mexico," p. 78.

TABLE III-10
Tax Rebate Incentives for Manufactured Exports

National Content		Tax Refund Certificate	
From	To	Previous	Current
40%	49%	—	5.5%
50%	59%	5.5%	7.0%
60%	100%	11.0%	11.0%

Source: Price Waterhouse & Co., *Mexico*, supplement to *Doing Business in Mexico* (New York: Price Waterhouse & Co., 1976), p. 11.

home larger revenues in the 1980s—"if the present system can hold out until then." [90]

First, Mexico will require large amounts of foreign foodstuffs to complement its own inefficient food output and to feed its booming population. Significantly, these imports cost the Mexican consumer more under the revised peso exchange rate.

Second, the volume of imported capital goods—the bulk of Mexico's imports—has grown considerably in recent years and must continue to do so if Mexico is to avoid outright economic stagnation. To capitalize on its petroleum resources, for example, Mexico must necessarily import much foreign drilling and refinery equipment. In fact, the United States Department of Commerce has alerted United States exporters that "capital goods, particularly in the priority areas of petroleum, iron and steel, and electrical power, will be in high demand," [91] and Mexican sources have themselves estimated that "machinery imports . . . could reach 15.2 billion dollars in the next five years." [92] In this respect, the effect of Mexico's devaluations on the country's balance of trade is somewhat self-defeating. Mexican exports cost less, but the imports on which Mexico's economy is desperately dependent now cost the country much more. As the *Wall Street Journal* observed:

> In theory, the peso float should be a threefold aid to the Mexican economy, boosting exports and tourism by making its goods and

---

[90] *Ibid.*

[91] U.S. Department of Commerce, *Foreign Economic Trends and Their Implications for the United States*, FET-75-052 (Washington, D.C.: U.S. Government Printing Office, 1975), p. 8.

[92] "Mexico—The Echeverría Years," p. 21.

services cheaper in relation to other currencies, and cutting imports by making them more expensive. . . .

But many economic observers doubt that such benefits will result. They say the nation's imports, mostly capital goods such as drilling rigs and machine tools to expand its industrial base and develop natural resources, can't be reduced without hampering economic growth. And they contend Mexico already is exporting at full capacity.[93]

A third consideration is that Mexican export sales are already hampered by high labor costs and inflation, both of which are escalating sharply. The upward direction of Mexico's inflation and wage trends will be reviewed later in this study in greater detail. It suffices to reiterate here that wage and price hikes tend to make Mexican export products more costly and reduce their competitiveness abroad. Trade reports have noted, for instance, that "Mexican exports to the United States grew only by 7.8 percent . . . [in 1975], and their prices reflected the relatively high rate of inflation that has afflicted Mexico since 1973." [94] Others have pointed out that 'steeply rising labor costs . . . put a crimp in [the] operations of . . . more than 500 "in-bond" plants that are allowed to import materials from the U.S. duty-free and export finished products back to the U.S.' [95] As Jorge Sanchez Mejorada, president of Mexico's Chamber of Industries, therefore concluded on the future of Mexico's foreign trade, "Everything will depend on what happens to wages and prices at home." [96]

INFLATION AND ITS CONTROL

Mexico entered 1977 with a low output of consumer durables, spiraling costs, and "the highest inflation since World War II"— an annual rate running above the 30 percent mark.[97] This last fact is particularly ominous since Mexico has historically *not* been an inflation-prone country. Between 1968 and 1972, for example, Mexico City's wholesale price index and the national consumer

---

[93] "Mexican Peso Declines as Much as 20% Against Dollar Following Float Decision," *Wall Street Journal*, September 2, 1976, p. 6.

[94] Riding, "Mexico Begins Export Offensive," p. C-58.

[95] "Winners and Losers as the Peso Floats," p. 36.

[96] Riding, "Mexico Begins Export Offensive," p. C-58.

[97] "Business Outlook—Mexico," p. 76.

price index rose by only 15.9 percent and 20.1 percent, respectively.[98] Mexico's prices and cost of living, however, escalated
sharply after 1972, pushing the country's rate of inflation to
record levels. By February 1977, Mexican wholesale prices were
up 167.9 percent over their 1970 level; consumer prices had
jumped by a crippling 144.3 percent during the same period.[99]

In 1975, then-President Echeverría delivered a four and a half
hour speech to the Mexican Congress, assuring the country's representatives that Mexico's consumer price index had increased by
only 10.1 percent between December 1973 and June 1974, and by
a lower 6.5 percent during the same period in 1974-75. Mexican
consumers, however, were already feeling a much stronger pinch
in their pocketbooks. According to Central Bank statistics, consumer prices rose by at least 23.7 percent throughout 1974 and
by 15 percent in 1975.[100] The national consumer price index was
27.2 percent higher in December 1976 than it had been in the
same month the previous year. At the same time:

> Wholesale prices in Mexico City rose an average 22.3% over the
> year, with the index ballooning 45.9% in the Dec. 1975-Dec. 1976
> comparison. (The official indices, however, include many items under
> price control. Labor unions and private sector organizations which
> run their own indices will be disputing the official data.)[101]

Several factors explain these onerous increases. According to
United States banking sources, much of Mexico's 1970 inflation
was attributed to such diverse cost pressures as "a poor crop
year for foodstuffs, higher prices of imports, relaxation of certain price controls . . . and higher labor costs resulting from
both a new labor law and a sharp rise in the minimum wage." [102]
The Inter-American Bank points out that inflation worsened in
1973, owing to an "upsurge in the price of imported petroleum
and derivatives, food products, raw materials and capital goods,
together with an inadequate domestic supply of certain foodstuffs

---

[98] Inter-American Development Bank, *Economic and Social Progress*, p. 343.

[99] International Monetary Fund, "Mexico," *International Financial Statistics*, Vol. XXX, No. 5 (May 1977), p. 279.

[100] *Mexico*, Economist Intelligence Unit QER No. 2 (London: EIU, 1976),
p. 7.

[101] The Mexican Chamber of Commerce of the United States, Inc., "Monthly
Digest," No. 815 (April 1977), p. 5.

[102] Ronald A. Krieger, *Mexico: An Economic Survey* (New York: First
National City Bank, 1971), p. 4.

FIGURE III-4
Cost of Living and Wholesale Price Trends

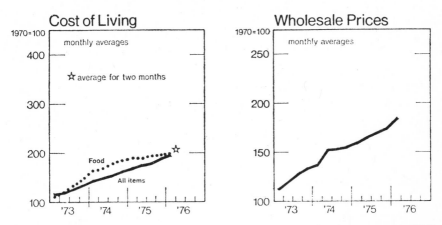

Source: *Mexico,* Economist Intelligence Unit QER No. 3 (London: EIU, 1976), p. 10.

and basic inputs needed by industry to meet the increased demand caused by larger public outlays." [103]

By the mid-1970s, then, it became clear that at least three factors—heavy government spending, high import prices, and high labor costs—were the main catalysts behind Mexico's snowballing inflation. Mexico's government aggravated the situation considerably by increasing continually the money supply after 1972 to meet the specie demand caused by higher wages. The net result, as one respected 1977 business report observed, was that

> The amount of bills and coins in circulation doubled in 1976, Mexico City wholesale prices raced upward at a 45.9% clip and the peso price of imports has increased. . . . These price pressures will lead to an unprecedented COL [cost of living] leap in 1977.[104]

Put simply, Mexico is in the grip of a wage-price spiral which is having a dangerous impact on the country's economy and political system alike. Spiraling wage and price hikes are hurting tourism, reducing the competitiveness of Mexican exports, and encumbering government efforts to improve the balance of payments. In the words of the Mexican Chamber of Commerce, "By 1976, Mexico had priced itself out of the world market for

---

[103] Inter-American Development Bank, *Economic and Social Progress,* p. 343.

[104] "Business Outlook—Mexico," p. 76.

many of its production items. . . . Domestic demand was slacken-
ing almost to a standstill as inflation had eroded the buying
power of a large segment of the population." [105]

The political impact of inflation in Mexico is no less critical.
Inflation accentuates trade union pressures for higher wages
and causes Mexico political, as well as economic, difficulties.
In a scramble for higher and faster wage adjustments, many
workers are coming to odds with the PRI's semiofficial labor
leadership. Their dissent is eroding the PRI's vital labor support and, as a result, the *de facto* stability of Mexico's political
system. ' "The guage is the stomach of the workers," ' the PRI's
labor spokesman and Mexico's national labor leader, Fidel
Velázquez, recently cautioned, ' "and when they have nothing
to eat, they won't respect any agreement and will fight to improve their situation, with or without the backing of their
leaders." ' [106]

In an effort to counter inflation, then, Mexico's government
has resorted to a series of monetary and fiscal moves which include federal budget cuts, new taxes, a freeze on credit, as well
as wage and price controls. It is most significant, however,
that few of these measures enhance the PRI's alliance with
organized labor. This is because Mexico's high inflation rate
and extensive foreign debt prompted the International Monetary
Fund to "urge" the government to curb inflation in Mexico at
all costs. Specifically, Mexico's government is under IMF pressure to bring inflation down to United States levels by 1979
and to reduce its budget deficit from 1976's 11.5 percent of the
gross national product to just 2.5 percent also by 1979. [107] The
result, as previously noted, is that federal spending for new
projects and for the repayment of public sector domestic debts
is being delayed.

New taxes are also in effect. Since 1974, they include a 15
percent tax on meals in Mexico's better restaurants, a 50 percent tax on gasoline sales, as well as higher taxes on car sales
and on income in excess of US$1,000 per month. Similarly, the
per annum cost of credit has been increased from 18 to 24 percent and a temporary freeze on credit for auto buyers is cur-

---

[105] The Mexican Chamber of Commerce of the United States, Inc., "Monthly
Digest," No. 815 (April 1977), p. 4.

[106] Riding, "Mexico's Inflation Fight: Stomach vs. Program," p. 33.

[107] The terms of Mexico's understanding with the IMF are highlighted
in the Alan Riding article cited above.

rently in effect. Explained one financial officer of Ford's Mexican affiliate, ' "Sales have been very slow since September [1976] . . . mainly because no credit is available. Dealers can only sell for cash." ' [108] Finally, Mexico's wage and price controls and currency float were implemented to counter inflation and its effects with even greater vigor.

Devaluation

Not an inflation "control" per se, devaluation has recently become a critical corollary of Mexican inflation. For twenty-two years, Mexico's government maintained a fixed exchange rate between pesos and dollars. "The peso," government officials touted in August 1976, "is the backbone for the strong and growing Mexican economy. While other currencies have not been able to maintain their parity with the U.S. dollar, the peso has proved extremely dependable, maintaining its parity at 12.5 pesos to the U.S. dollar, without interruption since the early 1950s." [109] On August 31, 1976, however, the peso exchange rate suddenly changed following a surprise government decision to float the currency. Within days, the dollar value of the peso plummeted from US$.08 to US$.049. On October 27, 1976, the government refloated Mexico's currency, allowing it to drop to an even lower 26.5 pesos to the dollar. These two adjustments effectively devalued Mexico's currency by some 52 percent.[110]

The Echeverría administration—in power at the time of both devaluations—was quick to launch an international press campaign to justify its exchange action. "The recent decision to float the peso," one government advertisement in a United States publication explained, ". . . follows the trend of international monetary policy. It recognizes current realities in the world marketplace, while serving, in effect, to make Mexican-made goods more competitive." [111] Mexico's Finance Secretary, Mario Ramon Beteta, was more specific when he acknowledged that the peso floats were aimed at reversing the heavy flight of capi-

108 Thomas E. Mullaney, "Optimism and Hope on Outlook in Mexico," *New York Times*, December 17, 1976, p. D-11.

109 "Mexico—The Echeverría Years," p. 26.

110 Alan Riding, "Mexico Lets Peso Slide 24.9% More in New Devaluation," *New York Times*, October 28, 1976, p. 61.

111 Director General de Informacion, "Mexico, Today and Tomorrow," p. 9.

tal and the decline in export and tourism revenues that had occurred because of continuing inflation.[112] This rationale was also expressed by the Mexican Chamber of Commerce and Mexico's Central Bank. The two peso floats, these latter sources made clear, were implemented to counter Mexico's export, tourism, and capital problems that "a vicious circle of increased demand, production bottlenecks and inflation had touched off." [113]

At the time of this writing, the peso continues to be a floating currency, undergoing as many as nine price changes in Mexico City in a single day. Mexico's inflationary spiral may actually offset the benefits of the recent devaluation. The implication is that steady devaluations of the peso are likely unless the government can drastically abate Mexico's inflation rate soon. This latter prospect is slim. As one senior economist at Chase Econometrics concluded, ' "We expect the value of the peso to be adjusted downward at relatively frequent intervals." ' [114]

Price Controls

Prices are largely regulated by the federal government in Mexico and have been for several decades. Simultaneously, Mexico's government has long sought to encourage agricultural production by maintaining price supports for various food products and has attempted to control the prices charged the public for these and other consumer goods in a variety of ways. Beginning in the 1950s, for example, stores operated by the government's National Company of Popular Subsistences (*Compañía Nacional de Subsitencias Populares*—CONASUPO) were opened to the public where staples—beans, corn, and other basic foods—could be purchased at very low prices. Rent and other more direct controls have also long been prevalent. Significantly, these direct controls have been greatly intensified in recent years.

In October 1974, President Echeverría decreed a rigid system of price regulations which froze the prices of 29 staple foods and consumer goods and put 170 other products under strict price control. These controls have affected greatly the pricing

---

[112] "Mexican Peso Declines as Much as 20% Against Dollar Following Float Decision," p. 6.

[113] The Mexican Chamber of Commerce of the United States, Inc., "Monthly Digest," No. 815 (April 1977), p. 4.

[114] Shaffer, "Mexico: More Troubles Ahead?," p. 24.

of chemicals, metals, clothes, appliances, and automobiles. "Together with the system of regulating the prices of food products and other consumer goods," Echeverría later explained, "a mechanism fixing prices to costs was implemented on October 3, which authorizes a proportional price increase when firms prove that their costs have increased by 5 percent or more." [115] As Mexico-watchers further noted:

> In a preamble to the decree, Echeverría said his objective was to "protect the purchasing power of the weakest sectors of the country, which are the ones most severely affected by inflation." Observers said he sought to protect the real value of 22% wage increases granted to Mexico's workers September 13. [116]

Today, Mexico's price controls can roughly be categorized into two groups. [117] Foodstuffs, soft drinks, all medicines, cigarettes, and petroleum-derived fuels are currently subject to rigid price control. Their prices were frozen at September 1974 levels and can only be changed after lengthy (and reluctant) federal investigations of profit, cost, and demand statistics. As appropriate, the government's National Company of Popular Subsistences may buy or sell large volumes of some of these items to adjust the market demand for them.

Prices for other products subject to the second, less stringent brand of control can be changed in proportion to cost increases, provided that companies submit proof to the Department of Industry and Commerce that their operating costs have increased by 5 percent or more. Manufacturers, wholesalers, and retailers with sales above specific peso volumes have been called on to report their selling prices. This information is the basis for the cost-increase tabulations and subsequent petitions to federal authorities for price increments.

Thus, price controls in Mexico are quite extensive. They are not at all easy to circumvent. A United States government survey has pointed out, for instance, that even a street musicians' union in Mexico City recently had to request permission to raise the price of a song from fifteen to twenty pesos. [118] During the

---

[115] Echeverría Álvarez, *Quinto Informe de Gobierno*, p. 41.

[116] Sobel, ed., *Latin American 1974*, p. 132.

[117] Information on Mexico's current price control system is taken from Price Waterhouse & Co., *Doing Business in Mexico*, pp. 19-21. Readers interested in further detail on this subject are urged to consult that study.

[118] Weil *et al.*, *Area Handbook*, p. 185.

first five days following Mexico's 1976 devaluations—which prompted panic price increases throughout the country—more than 500 stores were closed for price-control violations. Authorizations for price changes via the legal channels are complex and slow. They frequently do little to offset faster wage increases. In 1976, Volkswagen workers in Mexico struck for and won a 20 percent pay boost shortly before the government decreed an overall wage increase of 23 percent.[119] The government followed up, however, with a blanket 10 percent boost in the price of cars—an increase which was definitely "not . . . enough to offset higher costs and the effects of Mexico's . . . devaluation of the peso."[120] Indeed, the overall impact on Mexico's auto industry was so devastating that on June 20, 1977, López Portillo lifted the rigid price controls and loosened production limits for the auto industry. Similar action is now expected in other industries as well. As VW officials and other multinational businessmen can attest, however, price controls are still taken very seriously in Mexico.

Wage Controls

Wages increase through federally decreed minimum wages in Mexico and have traditionally been subject to government control via the PRI's close alliance with organized labor. Provisions for the establishment of minimum wages were first promulgated in Mexico's Constitution of 1917. After 1962, minimum wages were typically set once every two years on a regional and on an occupational basis by commissions composed of equal numbers of worker, employer, and government representatives. In September 1974, however, Mexico's federal labor law governing wage minimums was amended "as a result of nearly two years of a relatively high rate of inflation."[121]

Today, minimum wages are determined annually in Mexico for eighty occupations and eighty-nine geographic "wage zones." These minimums are set by tripartite Regional Minimum Wage Commissions—one for each zone—and ratified (or modified) by a tripartite National Minimum Wage Commission. The final

---

[119] "Mexico—VW Talks Merger with the Government," p. 48; "Mexico's Wage-Price Policy To Add to Inflationary Woes and Concerns Over Peso," *Business Latin America*, September 29, 1976, p. 305.

[120] "Mexico—VW Talks Merger with the Government," p. 48.

[121] Price Waterhouse & Co., *Doing Business in Mexico*, p. 52.

adjustment rulings of the National Commission supersede all collective contracts and are the basis for virtually all subsequent wage demands. As one United States Department of Labor study on Mexico points out, "In most major industries, wages are well above the minimum rates. Raising the minimum, however, does tend to elevate all wages, as workers generally demand wage raises commensurate with the increase over the old minimums." [122] In other words, minimum wage increments set the pace for all wage increases nationwide.

In this respect, Mexican wage increases are generally under substantial government control. Minimum wages are ostensibly determined by the government in Mexico in that the labor and government representatives on the minimum wage committees are PRI appointees who comprise a powerful voting bloc. Very recently, for example, United States embassy spokesmen in Mexico related:

> An employer member of the tripartite National Minimum Wage Commission said that the employer representatives had voted against the [1976] increases in 66 of the 89 economic zones of the country. Finally, Secretary of Labor, Carlos Galvez Betancourt, discouraged further commentary by saying that the new rates were within the "possibility of our economy", that they were not inflationary, that they would stimulate increases in production thereby creating new sources of employment.[123]

It is by virtue of this control over minimum wage increases that Mexico's PRI government has considerable control over wage increases in general.

Of course, the brace underlying this "control" is the government's long-standing alliance with Mexican labor. One United States labor specialist who spent a number of years in Mexico has pointed out that "the PRI's close relationship with organized labor is one of the government's main tools for controlling inflation." [124] To maintain this close relationship, however, minimum wages have typically been increased by the government so as to sustain the purchasing power of Mexican workers as well as to enhance the prestige of the government's semiofficial labor arm, the Mexican Workers' Confederation

---

[122] U.S. Department of Labor, *Labor Law and Practice in Mexico*, p. 45.

[123] American Embassy, Mexico, Airgram No. A-002 on Minimum Wage Statistics, January 9, 1976, U.S. Department of State, Washington, D.C.

[124] Author's conversation with John O'Grady, Latin-American labor authority, U.S. Department of State.

(*Confederación de Trabajadores de México*—CTM). As a result, a very complex wage adjustment ritual evolved in Mexico that became an integral part of the country's political and economic works.

It is believed that, until very recently, government and CTM labor officials convened prior to the meetings of the minimum wage commissions to agree upon the minimum wage increases that were to be decreed. To reiterate, these adjustments were generally geared to offset the impact of inflation on the working man's purchasing power. Once a new minimum range was established, CTM spokesmen publicly called for much higher wage increases, announcing that a general strike would be called unless its demands were met. The business community was invariably shaken by this threatened militancy since any strike in Mexico is usually a very serious ordeal. But after the minimum wage commissions met, the PRI's originally agreed-upon adjustments were finally decreed. They were higher than the increases management would otherwise have endorsed, but much lower than the exorbitant rates publicly demanded by labor. In this way, Mexican salaries escalated upward much to the satisfaction of Mexico's workers. The CTM gained prestige as the forceful bargaining agent of Mexican labor; employers were at least relieved that even higher wages were not granted; and the government cultivated labor support, asserting a kind of paternalistic dominion over the labor sector. As one Mexican businessman put it:

> Wage adjustments became a skillfully choreographed display of government and labor cooperation. Well, the ruling party's labor group—the CTM—rarely declared the general strike that it threatened. But the façade kept everyone happy and was all part of the political game.[125]

A look at the minimum wage adjustments authorized during the 1970s shows how this subtle wage control actually worked and, more importantly, how it was dangerously altered in recent years by higher and higher inflation. Statistics on Mexico's minimum wage adjustments are provided in Table III-11. In 1973, the Mexican Workers' Confederation (CTM) threatened a nationwide strike to back its demand for a 20 percent emergency pay increase. A week-long strike did take place in September 1973, after which workers won the full 20 percent jump

---

[125] Notes from author's conversations with Monterrey businessmen, April 15, 1977, Philadelphia, PA.

TABLE III-11
Minimum Wage Adjustment Trends, 1946-47 to 1974-75,
Simple Arithmetic Averages from All Wage Zones
(12.49 Pesos = US$1.00)

	URBAN			RURAL		
Biennial Periods	Pesos	% Compared Prior Biennial	Simple Index Base 1946-47= 100%	Pesos	% Compared Prior Biennial	Simple Index Base 1946-47= 100%
1946-47	2.48	—	100.0	2.05	—	100.0
1948-49	3.01	21.4	121.4	2.40	17.1	117.1
1950-51	3.35	11.3	135.1	2.66	10.8	129.8
1952-53	5.35	59.7	215.7	4.55	71.1	220.0
1954-55	6.34	18.5	255.6	5.26	15.6	256.6
1956-57	7.25	14.4	292.3	5.99	13.9	292.2
1958-59	8.13	12.1	327.8	6.86	14.5	334.6
1960-61	9.89	21.6	398.8	8.83	28.7	430.7
1962-63	12.44	25.8	501.6	10.92	23.7	532.7
1964-65	16.00	28.6	645.2	13.47	23.4	657.1
1966-67	18.69	16.8	753.6	15.72	16.7	766.8
1968-69	21.58	15.5	870.2	18.32	16.5	893.7
1970-71	24.91	15.4	1,004.4	21.20	15.7	1,034.2
1972-73	29.29	17.6	1,181.0	24.94	17.6	1,216.6
1973[a]	34.56	18.0	1,393.5	29.43	18.0	1,435.6
1974[b]	39.38	13.9	1,587.9	33.52	13.9	1,635.1
1974-75[c]	48.04	22.0	1,937.1	49.90	22.0	1,995.1

Source: American Embassy, Mexico, Airgram No. A-12 on Minimum Wage Statistics, January 12, 1976, U.S. Department of State, Washington, D.C.
[a] Minimum wages in force from Sept. 17 to Dec. 31, 1973.
[b] Minimum wages in force from Jan. 1 to Oct. 7, 1974.
[c] Minimum wages in force from Oct. 8, 1974, to Dec. 31, 1975.

that the CTM had demanded. The strike "threat" had become a reality. Months later in 1974, CTM President Fidel Velázquez called for an additional 35 percent emergency wage hike to "combat inflation's effect on salaries." [126] He again threatened

---

[126] Business International Corp., "Mexico," *Investing, Licensing, and Trading Conditions Abroad*, October 1975, p. 21.

to stage a general strike on September 20 if the new minimum wage boost were not decreed. Not surprisingly, a generous wage increase was negotiated (effective October 5) only one week before the CTM's deadline. The minimum wage for the federal district (Mexico City) jumped 24 percent from US $5.07 to US$6.29 for an eight-hour day. Nationwide, minimum wages were increased by an average 22 percent, and press reports pointed out that "Echeverria, who publicly supported the workers' demands, was credited with helping negotiate the 22% settlement." [127]

In 1976, Mexico's minimum wages were increased overall by 21 percent (January 1976), 23 percent (October 1976), and 9 percent (December 1976).[128] Even government analysts called 1976's 23 percent hike "unreasonable" because "it came on top of 15% to 20% raises obtained in contract negotiations a few weeks earlier in many industries." [129] The net result was that overall monthly earnings jumped 151 percent in Mexico during President Echeverría's administration (1970-1976),[130] adding considerably to the country's vicious wage-price spiral.

Clearly, the rapid, "unreasonable" wage increases authorized by the Echeverría regime sabotaged any semblance of federal wage control. Instead of fighting inflation by using the PRI's labor alliance to moderate wage hikes, Echeverría accelerated the practice of muffling labor's outcries against inflation with higher and faster wage adjustments. These wage gains only added to Mexico's inflationary spin and to labor's militancy. According to one press report:

> The 23 percent wage increase which followed the devaluation of the peso on August 31, and the mass expropriation of private farms in north-west Mexico . . . injected new militancy into . . . labour and peasant organisations.[131]

Under López Portillo, who took office in December 1976, Mexico's federal wage control tactics changed markedly. Concerned

---

[127] Sobel, ed., *Latin America 1974*, p. 132.

[128] "Mexico's New Minimum Wages," *Business Latin America*, January 7, 1976, p. 7; Arthur B. Nixon, U.S. Labor Attaché to Mexico, to the author, February 23, 1977.

[129] Shaffer, "Mexico: More Troubles Ahead?," p. 24.

[130] International Monetary Fund, "Mexico," *International Financial Statistics*, Vol. XXX, No. 5 (May 1977), p. 279.

[131] Alan Riding, "Mending the Broken Bridges," p. 7.

with the high level of inflation and under considerable pressure from labor, as well as from the International Monetary Fund, to bring the country's inflation rate down rapidly, López Portillo was forced to impose hard-line wage controls. ' "I want to study all the options, so don't push me up against the wall," ' the president told striking doctors in late 1976. ' "If it were only a matter of resolving your problems, it would be easy for me to give way. But what would happen to the wage structure of the rest of the country? We have to find solutions that do not simply create more problems and lead the country into chaos." ' [132]

López Portillo's solution, shortly after his election, was to persuade Fidel Velázquez and other PRI-loyal labor leaders to hold wage increases under a 10 percent ceiling through 1977. Once again, labor's close relationship with Mexico's dominant political party was the backbone of this control ploy. The government's wage control gamble was that "the semiofficial Mexican Workers Confederation . . . [would] maintain discipline in the labor movement until economic expansion . . . [could] be resumed." [133] But as diplomatic sources in Mexico City cautiously noted:

> Present signs indicate that organized labor will give the new President about six months of peace unless they experience another sharp rise in living costs. Mexican retailers and wholesalers have also pledged to hold prices in line. We'll see.[134]

The 10 percent wage ceiling lasted until August 3, 1977. President López Portillo, responding to extreme pressure from the prolabor leftist faction within the ruling PRI, dropped the guideline while acknowledging that inflation had increased almost 25 percent annually and, at the same time, putting pressure on the business community to expand private investment, to reduce profits, and to control prices.[135]

This antibusiness tone alarmed the business community; and on August 24, 1977, Mexico's major business organizations an-

---

[132] Alan Riding, "Lopez Portillo's Struggle," *Financial Times*, December 18, 1976, p. 5.

[133] Alan Riding, "Mexico's Conservatives Regaining Strength Since Lopez Took Office," *New York Times*, May 27, 1977, p. A-22.

[134] Arthur B. Nixon, U.S. Labor Attaché to Mexico, to the author, February 23, 1977.

[135] "Mexican Abandonment of 10% Wage Hike Ceiling Reveals Several Pressures," *Business Latin America*, August 10, 1977, p. 251.

nounced a ten-point plan in a "bid to cure the country's economic ills."[136] The ten points include the following:

1. A special bonus equal to fifteen days legal minimum wage in each geographic zone for permanent workers, which must be paid before November 1, 1977;

2. Employers are to establish a six-month training course for unemployed persons and pay them the minimum wage. The number of persons to be trained will be 2 percent of the individual company's workforce;

3. A resistance to price-hikes for 1977;

4. A promise not to pass along these new costs to consumers;

5. Private and partially state-owned banking institutions will establish credit packages for small and medium-size business;

6. A reinvestment pledge;

7. A pledge by companies to push export and import substitution;

8. A 10 percent decrease in export insurance premiums;

9. Stimulation of the production and distribution of low-cost basic goods; and finally,

10. Free advertising to be supplied to cooperating businesses by the radio and television stations.[137]

This voluntary program has extensive political overtones; and although it will have a monetary impact on business, it will not really alter the country's economic position.

The Impact of Mexico's Anti-Inflation Policies

Mexico's inflation controls have made very limited headway in slowing down the country's wage-price spiral. To be sure, some of the fury of the country's inflationary cycle is being abated. Retail and wholesale prices have, however, grown by at least 13 percent each year since 1974. They are likely to continue doing so throughout this decade because Mexico's inflation

---

[136] "Mexico's Businesses Pledge to Freeze Consumer Prices and to Pay Workers Bonus," *Wall Street Journal*, August 24, 1977, p. 11.

[137] "Developments in Mexico Point to Success of Political Juggling Act," *Business Latin America*, August 24, 1977, p. 266.

controls evidence several significant failings. They are counter-productive on several counts, being economically, as well as politically, damaging.

For example, Mexico's effective devaluations of the peso in 1976 were allegedly aimed at facilitating greater export and tourism revenues and at bringing back some of the capital that had fled the country in prior years. These reverses, Mexican officials believed, would strengthen the country's economy, thereby helping the federal battle against inflation. But the fact is that Mexico's devaluations of the peso were the result of—not any cure for—the country's unchecked inflationary drive. They have added considerably to Mexico's overall economic problems.

It was noted earlier that the peso devaluations have improved export sales. They have, however, made the cost of Mexico's imports soar—one prominent *cause* of inflation in the country—and have provoked major domestic price hikes at the same time. Days after the government's announcement of the exchange rate change, for instance, local department stores raised their prices "by as much as 30 percent." [138] The impact was perhaps especially acute in Mexico's auto industry. According to one 1977 United States business report:

> The rapid [exchange rate] change sent the cost of imported goods, including auto parts, soaring and helped boost the country's inflation rate. . . . The result was that auto companies' costs rose immediately—and then rose further as labor tried to catch up with higher wages—while the car market shriveled as the government slapped on such anti-inflation measures as tight credit. . . .
> Since the peso crumbled, new car sales have dropped by one-third, the industry's costs have outdistanced the average 48% increase in car prices, and layoffs have idled an estimated 20,000 out of 170,000 workers. [139]

Thus, the first of three important repercussions of Mexico's devaluations is that import prices have increased precipitously, heaping an added financial burden on Mexico's import-dependent economy. Second, labor attempts to "catch up" following the peso's plunge have been a veritable anathema to Mexico's anti-inflation efforts. As one United States labor specialist in Mexico City affirmed, "The [devaluation] action . . . created considerable

---

[138] Alan Riding, "Peso Tumbles 39% as Trading Resumes," *New York Times*, September 3, 1976, p. D-5.

[139] "Mexico: Why the Automakers Are Taking a Beating," *Business Week*, May 2, 1977, p. 41.

chaos in employer-labor relationships. The government increased wages in October [1976] by 23 percent and . . . [by] nine percent in late December." [140] Third, the switch to a free-floating exchange rate has eliminated one of Mexico's important investment attractions. No longer can the country claim the "attraction to investors that no other major Latin American country can match—a currency that is freely convertible at a fixed rate." [141]

Mexico's price controls have also shown several critical weaknesses. According to local businessmen, much of the impact of Mexican price controls is lost "due to the country's extensive black market activities." [142] Price controls are widely violated in Mexico and have been since the 1950s. Furthermore, state-controlled firms are typically the first to initiate price escalations. The Inter-American Bank has pointed out that "the prices and rates of several decentralized enterprises and agencies were raised in late 1973 in order to reduce . . . their deficits." [143] The Economist Intelligence Unit further noted that state-owned railways, interstate bus and road transport companies, and airlines all applied for rate increases in 1976 which would "push up prices across the board." [144] In fact, the tight finances of these companies left the government little margin for insistence on containing prices. By mid-1976, higher telephone and sugar prices were permitted—again at the bequest of state-controlled firms—along with several price hikes in the government-controlled energy field.[145]

In other words, price ceilings are hard to hold in Mexico's rather centralized economy. "Had unrealistically low prices been maintained," government officials stated concerning recent price increases among state-controlled enterprises, "the government

---

[140] Arthur B. Nixon, U.S. Labor Attaché to Mexico, to the author, February 23, 1977.

[141] "Latin America Opens the Door to Foreign Investment Again," p. 38.

[142] Notes from author's conversation with Monterrey businessmen, April 15, 1977, Philadelphia, PA.

[143] Inter-American Development Bank, *Economic and Social Progress*, p. 344.

[144] *Mexico*, Economist Intelligence Unit QER No. 2 (London: EIU, 1976), p. 7.

[145] Data on the price increases initiated by state-controlled firms are taken from "Mexico—The Echeverría Years," pp. 26-27; and *Mexico*, Economist Intelligence Unit QER No. 3 (London: EIU, 1976), pp. 4-6.

ould have had to provide subsidies, thus removing essential
nds from public services." [146]

Of all of Mexico's anti-inflation measures, however, the hard-
ne wage control which López Portillo tried to implement was
nquestionably the most important and controversial. Organized
abor is a key political ally of Mexico's long-ruling Institutional
evolutionary Party, the PRI, so that *de facto* wage controls are
lso very hard to impose. But as recent publications on Mexico
ow affirm, "Government economists believe nevertheless that
he key to controlling inflation is to limit wage increases." [147]
abor spokesmen challenge this stand on the ground that wages
re typically adjusted only once every twelve months in Mexico,
while industry and commerce set higher prices three or four
imes each year. Labor has publicly criticized the government's
minimum wage increases since 1975 as being ' "completely in-
ufficient." ' [148]

A look at the facts, however, proves that, until very recently,
Mexican wages have increased faster than the national consumer
price index throughout the early 1970s. To cite again United
States embassy spokesmen in Mexico City:

> The general impression here . . . is that organized workers have
> gained considerably in terms of real wages during the past six
> years. The same cannot be said for the rural sector workers.[149]

In other words, Mexican wage adjustments—at least for organized workers in nonagricultural activities—do appear to be
more than adequate. Wages were consistently increased above
observed price gains between 1969 and 1975, as Table III-12
and Figure III-5 make clear. Table III-12 also indicates that
increases in real minimum wages actually exceeded increases in
real *per capita* gross domestic product in 1972, 1974, and 1975.
Following the peso's devaluations in 1976, moreover, wages were
further hiked up by 23 percent in October and again by 9 percent
in December of that year. By year-end 1976, Mexico's wage increases had tallied a 122 percent gain over 1969 wage levels.

---

[146] "Mexico—The Echeverría Years," p. 26.

[147] Riding, "Mexico's Conservatives Regaining Strength Since Lopez Took
Office," p. A-22.

[148] Mexican labor's arguments for higher wages are discussed in American
Embassy, Mexico, Airgram No. A-002.

[149] Arthur B. Nixon, U.S. Labor Attaché to Mexico, to the author, February
23, 1977.

TABLE III-12
A Comparison of Mexico's Minimum Wage and
Consumer Price Increases
(1969 = 100)

Year	(1) Minimum Wage	(2) Consumer Price Index	(3) Real Minimum Wage (1÷2)	(4) Real Per Capita GDP
1970	115.4	105.0	109.9	103.2
1971	115.4	110.7	104.7	101.7
1972	135.7	116.2	116.8	105.4
1973	141.8	130.2	108.9	109.5
1974	192.5	161.2	119.4	112.0
1975	222.6	185.5 e	120.0 e	112.4 e

Source: American Embassy, Mexico, Airgram No. A-12 on Minimum Wage
          Statistics, January 12, 1976, U.S. Department of State, Washington,
          D.C.
      e   Estimate.

These kinds of "wage controls" left Mexico's government in a
very precarious position. On the one hand, the government placated industrial workers with wage adjustments that were anything but anti-inflationary, so that Mexican workers expected
and *demanded* wage increases that "protected" their purchasing
power. On the other hand, spiraling costs, economic mayhem,
and IMF insistence on financial discipline forced the López Portillo administration to take a remarkable stand.

Shortly after he took office, López Portillo persuaded PRI
labor leaders to accept a 10 percent limit on wage increases
throughout 1977. With inflation running about 30 percent, however, rebellion among the rank and file became apparent soon
after the agreement. As pointed out earlier, this 10 percent
limit remained in effect until August 3, 1977. In February 1977,
2,500 workers at General Motors' Mexico City plant struck for
a 24 percent wage increase.[150] The shutdown was organized by

---

[150] Information on the strikes following labor's 1976 agreement on the 10
percent wage-adjustment ceiling was taken from: Alan Riding, "Mexico's
Inflation Fight: Stomach vs. Program," p. 33; "GM Says Strike at Plant
in Mexico City Is Ended," *Wall Street Journal*, April 13, 1977, p. 11; and
Alberto Gomez Obregon, Personnel Director of Labor, interview held at
General Motors plant, Mexico City, August 24, 1977.

FIGURE III-5
A Comparison of Monthly Earnings and Consumer Price Trends in Mexico (1970 = 100)

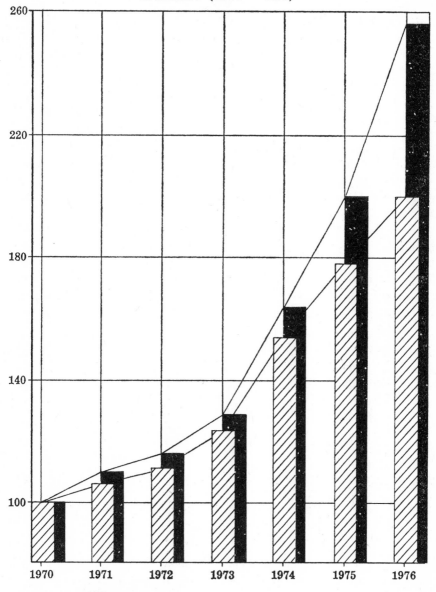

■ Monthly Earnings

⧸⧸⧸ Consumer Prices

Source: International Monetary Fund, "Mexico," *International Financial Statistics*, Vol. XXX, No. 5 (May 1977), p. 279.

an independent union and lasted sixty-two days. It was only settled after GM agreed to a wage increase of 10 percent (retroactive to February at 50 percent). In March, workers at the state-controlled Altos Hornos steel complex struck for one week before accepting a 10 percent wage increase plus similarly costly fringe benefits. At the very same time, the federal electricity commission's union mobilized for a 16 percent wage raise.

These examples make clear that inflation, on the one hand, and hard-line wage controls, on the other, are eroding the government's control over organized labor. Strikes for better wages and fringe benefits are now being organized despite the CTM's hold-off pledge. As a result, the PRI is losing some of its vital labor support. CTM President Fidel Velázquez has attempted to counter the rank and file's dissent by announcing that his Confederation will seek an "escalator clause in collective contracts which will grant automatic wage increases in line with increases in the cost-of-living index if prices continue to rise." [151] Nevertheless, many workers—already experiencing a drop in their living standard and disgruntled with the PRI "solidarity" tactics they now see practiced—are defecting from Mexico's traditional, PRI-dominated unions to join militant splinter groups. As recent studies confirm:

> New unions, independent of the CTM and other traditional groups, are seizing the opportunity to build support from the rank and file, often through demonstrations of increased militancy. The situation is obviously volatile. . . .[152]

To reiterate, then, Mexico's anti-inflation measures are either very weak or very damaging. Mexico's devaluations of the peso have heated—not cooled—inflation. Price controls are considerably ineffective (but nevertheless very painful) in Mexico's centralized economy, and the current administration's insistence on tighter wage control has placed Mexico's PRI government in a dangerous political and economic quandary. One equally vital assessment of the country's anti-inflation policies, however, is demonstrated by their impact on the multinational firms operating in Mexico. In the words of one analyst:

> Their sales have been reduced sharply. They have been affected by large increases in costs, especially wages. They have had difficulty in obtaining local credit. Some have had to shut down plants

---

[151] American Embassy, Mexico, Airgram No. A-002.

[152] "Mexico—The Next Five Years," p. 84.

temporarily. Almost all have had to reduce their work forces by 5 to 10 percent or more because of the long delays in obtaining Government approval for the price relief they say is needed. And the number of items placed under price control has recently been doubled to about 200.[153]

INCOME DISTRIBUTION AND WAGES

Until very recently, wages escalated rapidly in Mexico with the government's generous adjustments of minimum wages. Even so, Mexican wages are still very low by United States standards. For example, women employed in shrimp packaging firms on the Texas side of the border earn a base pay of US$2.30 an hour (US$2.12 an hour take-home) to grade and package shrimp with the help of machines. Female employees in nearby firms on the Mexican side of the border shell and clean shrimp by hand for US$.99 an hour (US$.65 an hour take-home).[154] The disparity is startling but typical.

Minimum wages in Mexico vary considerably from one geographic region and occupation to the next, and even Mexico's highest minimum wages are much lower than their United States counterparts. Tables III-13 and III-14 list the daily minimum wages in Mexico at the outset of 1977. These figures are official 1976 base minimum wages adjusted by 23 percent for the October 1976 emergency hike and by another 9 percent for the later December 1976 increase. They are presented by economic or wage zones and by basic occupations as stipulated by Mexican labor law.

As of January 1977, the daily minimum industrial wage in Baja California, Mexico's highest wage zone, was 133.80 pesos— *i.e.*, US$6.03 at the January exchange rate—for an eight-hour day. The comparable minimum rate in the Oaxaca-Guerrero area, Mexico's lowest wage zone, was 46.66 pesos—*i.e.*, US$2.10 a day or US$.26 an hour. Similarly, the daily minimum for auto and truck mechanics was 43 pesos or some US$2.00 higher in Baja California than that decreed for the same workers in Mexico City. These minimum wage disparities account for the sometimes great differentials in the pay given workers in different parts of the country for doing the very same job.

---

[153] Mullaney, "Optimism and Hope on Outlook in Mexico," p. D-11.

[154] James P. Sterba, "Cheap Mexican Labor Attracts U.S. Companies to the Border," *New York Times*, May 13, 1977, p. A-1.

TABLE III-13

January 1977 Minimum Daily Wages by Region

States and Economic Subregions	Industry Minimum (Pesos)	Rural Minimum (Pesos)
Aguascalientes	73.60	62.21
Baja California	133.80	105.51
Baja California Sur	100.95	83.26
Campeche		
Campeche Carmen	69.05	54.57
Campeche Centro	64.35	53.63
Campeche Norte .	53.63	49.74
Chiapas		
Chiapas Centro	51.62	43.30
Chiapas La Costa Tuxtla Chico	59.12	46.66
Chiapas Norte Pichucalco	66.10	52.29
Chiapas Palenque	47.72	40.76
Chiapas Tapachula	79.77	56.98
Chihuahua		
Chihuahua Chihuahua	91.30	83.39
Chihuahua Ciudad Juarez	111.28	97.33
Chihuahua Guerrero	80.44	67.84
Chihuahua Jimenez	83.39	66.90
Chihuahua Noreste	87.01	82.72
Chihuahua Sierra	80.44	67.43
Coahuila		
Cohuila Norte	94.25	70.39
Coahuila Monclova	93.98	70.39
Coahuila Oeste	64.89	57.78
Coahuila Saltillo	84.06	62.74
Comarca Lagunera	87.15	66.77
Nuevo Leon Norte	63.68	58.45
Colima	83.79	78.16
Durango		
Comarca Lagunera	87.15	66.77
Durango Centro	67.84	56.04
Durango Este	56.44	50.81
Durango Norte-Oeste-Sur	64.35	56.04
Guanajuato		
Guanajuato Centro	81.78	58.19
Guanajuato Michoacan Bajio	68.78	58.19
Guanajuato Norte	56.85	47.59
Guerrero		
Guerrero Acapulco	101.49	85.00
Guerrero Centro	60.60	48.13
Guerrero Chilpancingo Costa Grande	78.57	63.82
Guerrero Oaxaca La Costa	53.36	49.61
Michoacan Centro	87.68	80.31
Oaxaca Guerrero Mixteca	46.66	40.36

TABLE III-13—Continued

States and Economic Subregions	Industry Minimum (Pesos)	Rural Minimum (Pesos)
Hidalgo		
Estado de Mexico Noreste	81.51	63.42
Hidalgo	67.84	56.44
San Luis Potosi Sur Huastecas	78.03	72.67
Jalisco		
Colima	83.79	78.16
Guadalajara Metropolitan Area	95.19	88.75
Jalisco Bolanos Los Altos	61.81	54.16
Jalisco Centro Costa	75.75	71.33
Jalisco Ocotlan	85.00	79.24
Mexico		
Estado de Mexico Centro Sur	78.43	62.61
Estado de Mexico Este	89.83	73.74
Estado de Mexico Norte	69.58	53.09
Estado de Mexico Noreste	81.51	63.42
Estado de Mexico Toluca	91.03	68.24
Federal District Metropolitan Area	105.38	98.14
Michoacan		
Colima	83.79	78.16
Guanajuato Michoacan Bajio	68.78	58.19
Jalisco Centro Costa	75.75	71.33
Michoacan Centro	87.68	80.31
Michoacan Cienega de Chapala	82.72	77.22
Michoacan Costa	76.42	68.24
Michoacan Meseta Tarasca	72.00	60.20
Michoacan Morelia	83.79	68.24
Michoacan Zitacuaro	73.74	68.51
Morelos	88.22	77.09
Nayarit	68.38	65.16
Nuevo Leon		
Monterrey Metropolitan Area	99.48	93.18
Nuevo Leon Montemorelos	82.72	77.09
Nuevo Leon Norte	63.68	58.45
Nuevo Leon Sabinas Hidalgo	83.79	73.07
Nuevo Leon Sur	63.15	57.38
Oaxaca		
Guerrero Oaxaca La Costa	53.36	49.61
Oaxaca Centro	59.26	50.68
Oaxaca Guerrero Mixteca	46.66	40.36
Oaxaca Istmo	77.76	59.39
Oaxaca Tuxtepec	64.35	60.47

TABLE III-13—Continued

States and Economic Subregions	Industry Minimum (Pesos)	Rural Minimum (Pesos)
Puebla		
Puebla Centro Sur	81.25	71.86
Puebla Metropolitan Area	91.57	73.34
Puebla Sierra	76.96	66.36
Queretaro		
Queretaro Norte	50.28	41.43
Queretaro Queretaro	77.36	59.26
Queretaro Sur	60.73	48.53
Quintana Roo	89.56	89.56
San Luis Potosi		
San Luis Potosi Norte	58.86	50.28
San Luis Potosi Sur Huastecas	78.03	72.67
Sinaloa		
Sinaloa Norte	91.97	80.44
Sinaloa Noreste	84.46	75.88
Sinaloa Sur	84.46	73.47
Sonora		
Baja California Norte	133.80	105.51
Sonora Costa	92.51	88.22
Sonora Sierra	78.97	75.21
Sonora Nogales	104.57	95.19
Tabasco	80.44	62.88
Tamaulipas		
Tamaulipas Centro	78.30	64.09
Tamaulipas Mante	90.63	78.83
Tamaulipas Norte	107.93	89.83
Tamaulipas Tampico Madero Altamira	103.90	75.62
Tlaxcala	61.67	52.43
Veracruz		
San Luis Potosi Sur Huastecas	78.03	72.67
Veracruz Centro	90.50	75.88
Veracruz Minatitlan Coatzacoalcos	110.88	88.89
Veracruz Poza Rica Tuxpan	99.88	79.91
Yucatan		
Yucatan Agricola Forestal	61.94	56.85
Yucatan Merida Progreso	79.77	60.33
Zacatecas		
Zacatecas Centro	67.17	55.50
Zacatecas (rest of state)	59.53	49.87

Source: Alberto Trueba Urbina and Jorge Trueba Barrera, *Nueva Ley Federal del Trabajo Reformada* (Mexico: Editorial Porrua S.A., 1976).

Note: The figures in this table are the official 1976 base minimum wages adjusted by two wage increases—23 percent and 9 percent, respectively.

TABLE III-14
January 1977 Minimum Daily Wages by Occupation
(Dollar Equivalents Expressed at January 1977 Exchange Rate)

Occupation	Baja California Pesos	Baja California US$	Mexico City Pesos	Mexico City US$
Assistant Accountant	188.10	8.48	148.15	6.68
Assistant Laboratory Analyst	178.98	8.07	139.70	6.30
Auto Greaser	174.56	7.87	137.42	6.20
Auto/Truck Mechanic	202.58	9.14	159.54	7.19
Automotive Parts Clerk	176.30	7.95	138.90	6.26
Bartender/Canteen Keeper	177.24	7.99	139.57	6.29
Cashier	173.62	7.83	136.75	6.17
Chicken Farmer	167.32	7.55	131.79	5.94
Clerical Worker	173.62	7.83	136.75	6.17
Construction Carpenter	181.80	8.20	143.19	6.46
Cook/Chef	198.16	8.94	156.06	7.04
Crane/Derrick Operator	185.42	8.36	146.00	6.58
Drugstore/Pharmacy Clerk	170.00	7.67	133.94	6.04
Electrician (Cars/Trucks)	192.66	8.69	151.77	6.84
Electrician (Installations/Repairs)	190.78	8.60	150.29	6.77
Electrician (Motors/Generators)	185.42	8.36	146.00	6.58
Elementary School Teacher	206.20	9.30	162.49	7.33
Farm Machinery Operator	154.85	6.98	105.38	4.75
Furniture Maker	191.72	8.65	150.96	6.81
Gas Station Attendant	172.68	7.79	105.38	4.75
Hairdresser/Manicurist	181.80	8.20	143.19	6.46
Hotel Chambermaid	169.06	7.62	133.13	6.00
Lathe Operator	189.98	8.57	149.62	6.75
Linotypist	202.58	9.14	159.54	7.19
Master Mason	195.34	8.81	153.91	6.94
Metal Worker (Construction)	188.10	8.48	148.15	6.68
Milling Machine Operator	197.22	8.89	155.25	7.00
Mold Maker	185.42	8.36	146.00	6.58
Muffler Repairman	191.72	8.65	150.96	6.81
Night Watchman/Guard	172.68	7.79	136.08	6.14
Painter (Buildings)	186.36	8.40	146.67	6.61
Painter (Cars/Trucks)	188.10	8.48	148.15	6.68
Plumber	187.16	8.44	147.48	6.65

TABLE III-14—Continued

Occupation	Baja California		Mexico City	
	Pesos	US$	Pesos	US$
Print Composer	184.48	8.32	145.33	6.55
Receptionist	174.56	7.87	137.42	6.20
Registered Nurse	220.81	9.96	173.89	7.84
Repairman (Electric/Electronic)	194.54	8.77	153.11	6.90
Seamstress (Factory)	171.61	7.74	136.08	6.14
Shoemaker	175.36	7.91	138.09	6.23
Silversmith	181.80	8.20	143.19	6.46
Social Worker	216.25	9.75	170.27	7.68
Steam Boiler Operator	186.36	8.40	146.67	6.61
Stenographer-Typist	182.74	8.24	143.86	6.49
Tailor (Home Tailoring)	196.28	8.85	154.18	6.95
Tile/Mosaic Layer	190.78	9.60	150.29	6.78
Truck Driver	188.10	8.48	148.15	6.68
Warehouse Clerk	176.30	7.95	138.90	6.26
Woodworker	186.36	8.40	146.67	6.61

Source: Alberto Trueba Urbina and Jorge Trueba Barrera, *Nueva Ley Federal del Trabajo Reformada* (Mexico: Editorial Porrua S.A., 1976).
Note: The figures in this table are the official 1976 base minimum wages adjusted by two wage increases—23 percent and 9 percent, respectively.

Although Mexico's minimum daily wages are low when expressed in United States currency, the monthly and annual salaries that they yield are somewhat augmented by a series of wage bonuses. First, Mexican labor law requires that workers be paid for one day of rest for each six days on the job. Thus, a worker earning 100 pesos a day in Mexico actually receives 700 pesos for a six-day work week. Second, workers with more than one year's seniority are additionally entitled to six days or more of paid vacation [see "Working Conditions," pp. 91-94]. Year-end bonuses and supplemental payments in Mexico are also commonplace. According to one United States government report on Mexican wages:

> Supplemental payments (*prestaciones*) of various kinds are common for both production and office workers. One of the most common types of supplements is the yearend bonus (*aguinaldo*), usually paid at Christmas time. Occasionally, the yearly bonus is paid to

a worker immediately preceding his vacation or payment is divided among two or more holiday periods. Some companies grant from 1 week's to 1 month's (or more) extra pay as an annual bonus. Others base bonuses on a worker's annual wages, granting a 4, 8 or possibly 10 percent supplement at the end of the year. In still other companies, yearend bonuses are based on production, sales or profits . . . and punctuality records. . . .[155]

Finally, the collective contracts negotiated by management and organized labor usually establish wages above the minimums decreed by the government. The differential generally depends on the geographic location of the firm or plant and the militancy of the bargaining union. Examples of average monthly Mexican salaries as of mid-1976 are provided in Table III-15.

Nationwide, then, the number of Mexicans earning only minimum wages is rather hard to pinpoint. Mexican government agencies and the PRI-dominated local press are deliberately slow in releasing figures on the country's poor income distribution. Instead, local officials are quick to cite Mexico's *per capita* income figures—among the highest in Latin America—to depict the average wealth of the Mexican people. These statistics are accurate but very misleading.

In 1969, for example, Mexico's average annual *per capita* income was US$645. Almost 18 percent of Mexico's population, however, had annual incomes under US$75 that year.[156] In 1970, an estimated 2 percent of the economically active population had incomes over US$400 a month, while 42 percent received monthly incomes under US$40. United States government studies have also pointed out:

> In 1972 the minister of finance, in a statement calling for more equal distribution of wealth, contended that 10 percent of the population received 50 percent of the total income in the country while at the other extreme 50 percent of the population received only 10 percent of the income. Another study in 1972 revealed that annual rural per capita income was one-fourth the national average of the equivalent of US$744 and that the per capita income of the upper 30 percent of the population was equivalent to US$1,400, which was on par with per capita incomes of many industrialized nations.[157]

Although more recent statistics are not available at this time, Mexican government officials have hinted that 62 percent of

---

[155] U.S. Department of Labor, *Labor Law and Practice in Mexico*, p. 47.

[156] Weil *et al.*, *Area Handbook*, p. 276.

[157] *Ibid.*

TABLE III-15
Typical 1976 Monthly Salaries
(Pesos)

Occupation	Mexico City	Guadalajara	Monterrey
Entry Level or Starting Positions			
Chemical Engineer	6,177	5,500	6,063
Civil Engineer	6,206	7,000	6,038
Economist	5,879	—	6,214
Electrical-Mechanical Engineer	6,313	5,714	6,050
Industrial Engineer	6,290	5,833	6,000
MBA	10,442	—	7,813
Established Positions			
Computer Operator	5,841	5,050	4,100
General Manager	31,388	29,133	31,025
Head Accountant	14,867	12,818	13,262
Marketing Manager	22,443	—	—
Office Manager	22,060	20,295	20,808
Personnel Manager	17,370	14,608	17,119
Plant/Factory Manager	21,820	20,389	23,312
Sales Engineer	12,805	—	—
Senior Accounting Clerk	5,667	5,024	4,858
Shift Foreman "A"	8,195	7,008	7,506
Spanish-English Exec. Secretary	8,936	5,560	5,973
Typist	3,591	2,929	3,319
Warehouse Clerk	4,163	3,671	3,725

Source: "Compensation Study Reveals Important Data on Mexican Wage Patterns," *Business Latin America*, August 11, 1976, p. 254.

Mexico's population depends on minimum wages; average *per capita* figures aside, they acknowledge that income distribution in Mexico is extremely unbalanced. Simply stated, Mexico is a country of economically polarized "haves" and "have-nots" like most other Latin American republics. This fact, according to one United States Department of Commerce publication, is "one of . . . [Mexico's] chief obstacles to a higher rate of economic development." [158] In the words of former President Echeverría, ' "The excessive concentration of wealth and the existence of large groups of human beings living on the edge of productive society constitute a serious threat to our continued and harmonious development." ' [159] This concern—at least until very recently—undoubtedly added great impetus to the government's higher wage drive.

Poor income distribution has also been the catalyst for other problems in Mexico. Mexico's internal wage differences have prompted large-scale internal migrations which are resulting in urban overcrowding and rising unemployment. Rural discontent is also high because of the wage disparities. One recent study notes that the income of Mexico's landless peasants fell by 15 percent over a ten-year period, while that of factory workers increased by 20 percent. [160] In other words, the income polarization of Mexico's civil servants and industrial workers, on the one hand, and peasants, on the other, is becoming more pronounced. The result is that discontent is spreading throughout the agricultural sector, putting strong pressure on Mexico's government to redress the income distribution problem. But as one Mexican business executive cautioned:

> There is still, no doubt, a great deal of poverty in Mexico and the need for a more equitable distribution of wealth. However, we cannot go too fast in this process of redistribution through higher taxes, ceiling prices, and higher wages as otherwise we will end up by only distributing poverty. What we need mostly at the present time is to generate wealth and jobs through new industries and the modernization of farming. [161]

THE MEXICAN JOB MARKET

The creation of new jobs in Mexico is another critical government concern. Mexican unemployment and underemployment are already serious problems. Furthermore, the number of Mexicans without full-time or gainful employment is growing rapidly each

---

[158] U.S. Department of Commerce, *Establishing a Business in Mexico*, p. 2.

[159] Director General de Informacion, "Mexico, Today and Tomorrow," p. 9.

[160] Douglas A. Hellinger and Stephen H. Hellinger, *Unemployment and the Multinationals* (Port Washington: Kennikat Press, 1976), p. 14.

[161] Eduardo Prieto Lopez, "Labor and Management in Mexico," in *Seminar on Doing Business in Modern Mexico* (Berkeley: University of California at Berkeley, 1967), p. 62.

year. "There has been no improvement in the employment situation in recent years," the Inter-American Bank affirms. "The labor force, swollen by a large increase in population, has become a depressive factor in the economy since the people seeking work far outnumber . . . employment opportunities. This situation is aggravated by the age composition of the population and the prospect of continued expansion of the labor force."[162]

Most of Mexico's development has been capital—not labor—intensive. The broad industrial infrastructure that Mexico has built up over the years is not extremely conducive to absorbing additional manpower. Yet, Mexico's population is growing with great speed. The country's birth rate, 3.5 percent a year, is reputed to be one of the world's highest. Women, who typically did not work due to the country's hispanic work ethic, have also begun inflating the labor force in increasing numbers to supplement tight family incomes. In 1970, these growth factors led Mexican officials to project the need for between 500,000 and 600,000 new jobs each year. By 1976, spokesmen for the Mexican Employers' Federation estimated that 7.65 million new jobs would have to be created by 1982—roughly, 1 million new jobs a year—to accommodate Mexico's growing labor force.[163]

A look at Mexico's past employment trends puts these projections into grim perspective. Regrettably, accurate statistics on Mexican employment are not available. Table III-16 presents Mexican government figures for 1950 through 1975. These data, however, are unquestionably distorted. Government statistics only cover workers over the age of 12, even though respected Mexican university sources have estimated that at least 105,000 minors under that age limit were working in 1973.[164] Other authorities have suggested that the government's 1970 figures understate the number of Mexican workers by several million. The government counted 415,000 unemployed persons in Mexico, *i.e.*, 3.2 percent of the labor force, in 1970. Three years later, however, North American publications were reporting a 2.2 million, *i.e.*, 16 per-

---

[162] Inter-American Development Bank, *Economic and Social Progress*, p. 344.

[163] "News & Comments," *Business Trends*, Vol. X, No. 463 (December 1975), p. 2.

[164] Weil *et al.*, *Area Handbook*, p. 44. Note: TITLE ONE, ARTICLE 22 of Mexico's Reformed Federal Labor Law technically prohibits the employment of children under the age of 14 or of minors between the ages of 14 and 16 who lack express governmental and parental authorization.

TABLE III-16

Official Mexican Manpower Configurations, 1950-1975

Employment Breakdown	1950		1960		1970		1975 [f]	
	Thousands	Percent	Thousands	Percent	Thousands	Percent	Thousands	Percent
Total Population	25,791	100.0	34,923	100.0	48,255	100.0	60,145	100.0
Economically Active [a]	8,345	32.4	11,332	32.4	12,955	26.9	16,597	27.6
Economically Inactive	17,446	67.6	23,591	67.6	35,300	73.1	43,548	72.4
Economically Active	8,345	100.0	11,332	100.0	12,955	100.0	16,597	100.0
Employed	8,240	98.7	n.a.	n.a.	12,540	96.8	n.a.	n.a.
Unemployed	105 [b]	1.3	n.a.	n.a.	415	3.2	n.a.	n.a.
Total Labor Force by Industry	8,272 [c]	100.0	11,332	100.0	12,955	100.0	16,597	100.0
Agriculture, Forestry, Hunting, and Fishing	4,824	58.3	6,145	54.2	5,104	39.5	6,783	40.9
Mining and Quarrying	97	1.2	142	1.3	180	1.4	241	1.4
Manufacturing	973	11.8	1,556	13.7	2,169	16.7	2,961	17.8
Construction	225	2.7	408	3.6	571	4.4	756	4.6
Electricity	25 [d]	0.3	41	0.4	53	0.4	71	0.4
Commerce	684	8.3	1,075	9.5	1,197	9.2	1,654	10.0
Transport and Communications	211	2.5	357	3.2	369	2.8	490	3.0
Services (inc. gas, water, and sanitary services)	879	10.6	1,526	13.5	2,565	19.8	3,641	21.9
Activities not adequately described	355	4.3	82	0.7	748	5.8	—	—

Employment Breakdown	1950		1960		1970		1975 f	
	Thousands	Percent	Thousands	Percent	Thousands	Percent	Thousands	Percent
Total Labor Force by Occupational Group	8,272	100.0	11,332	100.0	12,955	100.0	16,597	100.0
Professional, Technical, and Related Workers	207	2.5	410	3.6	733	5.7	1,029	6.2
Administrative, Executive, and Managerial Personnel	65	0.8	95	0.8	320	2.5	432	2.6
Clerical Workers	385	4.7	693	6.1	977	7.5	1,346	8.1
Sales Workers	647	7.8	1,024	9.0	967	7.5	1,351	8.1
Service Workers (transport, communications, recreation)	594	7.1	793 e	7.0	1,560	12.0	2,184	13.2
Agricultural, Husbandry and Forestry Workers, Fishermen, etc.	4,812	58.2	6,065	53.6	4,724	38.2	6,525	39.3
Production Workers, Miners, and Laborers	1,562	18.9	2,142 e	18.9	2,769	21.4	3,729	29.5
Workers Not Classifiable by Occupation	—	—	—	—	676	5.2	—	—

Sources: International Labour Office, *Anuario de Estadisticas del Trabajo* (Geneva: ILO, 1971 and 1976); Thomas E. Weil et al., *Area Handbook for Mexico*, 2nd ed. (Washington, U.S. Government Printing Office, 1975); and U.S. Department of Labor, *Labor Law and Practice in Mexico* (Washington, D.C.: U.S. Government Printing Office, 1963).

Note: Because of rounding, sums of individual items may not equal totals.

a Economically active population figures relate to persons over the age of 12 who work.

b 1950 unemployment figures include workers unemployed for any length of time.

c 1950 total labor force excludes 73,000 persons unemployed for 13 weeks or more.

d 1950 electricity figure includes electric, gas, water, and sanitary services.

e 1960 service worker figures exclude transport and communications, which are included under production workers.

f Official government estimates.

cent, unemployment total for the country.[165] The Mexican Ministry of Labor sets the total unemployment and underemployment at 49 percent—unemployment at 9 percent and underemployment at 40 percent.[166] "Of every 10 working-age Mexicans," one United States publication has concluded, "four are unemployed or underemployed. Each year, 800,000 young people pour into the labor market, and the flood of job seekers will swell as the present population doubles by the year 2000."[167]

Underemployment, then, is also a very serious problem at this time. It is most prevalent in rural areas since Mexico's agricultural system is simply not adequate to support the country's many peasants—officially, some 40 percent of the labor force. According to one study of the problem, "Mexico provides an example of a country where rapid economic growth has been accompanied by an equally rapid growth in underemployment and where official rhetoric concerning the creation of more employment opportunities has not been matched by effective action."[168] Again, official and private estimates of underemployment differ considerably because underemployment is loosely defined. Even so, a 29 percent underemployment rate for Mexico is a reasonable, perhaps conservative estimate. In fact, organized labor frequently cites the underemployment problem in calling for a reduction of the work week from 48 to 40 hours, a key union demand.

The important fact, in any event, is that Mexican unemployment and underemployment already are acute. Their impact is abundantly evident in Mexico. Visitors there have reported, for example, that

> The streets are filled with the unemployed, some begging or desperately seeking income by shining shoes, offering goods of all kinds for sale and soliciting the passerby's business in many ways. Even a police officer on a main thoroughfare was trying to steer a tourist away from a department store for a friend's taxi ride to a nearby retail market.[169]

---

165 *Ibid.*, p. 46.

166 Arthur B. Nixon, Labor Attaché, interview at the United States Embassy, Mexico City, August 24, 1977.

167 "Time Bomb in Mexico," *U.S. News and World Report*, July 4, 1977, p. 27.

168 Hellinger and Hellinger, *Unemployment and the Multinational*, p. 116.

169 Mullaney, "Optimism and Hope on Outlook in Mexico," p. D-11.

Additionally, migrations by Mexico's peasants and jobless to urban centers and to the United States are escalating. Recent reports note that "every day—or night—hundreds, perhaps thousands, of Mexicans sneak across their country's 2,000 mile-long northern border to become illegal job hunters in the U.S. Already there are probably more than 6 million Mexicans living in the United States illegally." [170] Since 1965, the number of legal Mexican immigrants to the United States has doubled, although a new United States immigration law effective January 1, 1977, has cut the number of annual legal entries from Mexico for permanent residence down 50 percent to 20,000. Thus, legal access to the United States job market has been considerably narrowed.

These various facts illustrate the magnitude of the task ahead —that of creating jobs for a rapidly increasing labor force. The task is particularly difficult in that Mexican labor is chronically underskilled and does not lend itself to rapid development of labor-intensive activities. Managers of United States branch plants in Mexico report that "the Mexican worker is as productive as a worker in the United States if given adequate education and training, the same equipment, and the same working and dietary conditions." [171] But Mexican workers have limited formal educations. Most must be trained exclusively on the job since vocational training is relatively scarce. Publications provided by the American Chamber of Commerce of Mexico also point out:

> Most firms find labor plentiful and relatively cheap, although not very productive. A good many feel that their principal operating problem is the serious shortage of skilled labor and managerial personnel. . . .
> Absenteeism is a major problem. It tends to peak on Mondays, with about 25% of workers usually out. This drops substantially in mid-week, but may rise again to 20% on Fridays and Saturdays. A recent study by the Mexican Association of Finance Executives found that each Mexican worker loses an average of 12.5 working days a year.[172]

Thus, Mexico's employment problems are complex and critical and add to the country's overall economic malaise. They also

---

[170] "Time Bomb in Mexico," p. 27.

[171] U.S. Department of Labor, *Labor Law and Practice in Mexico*, p. 12.

[172] Business International Corp., "Mexico," *Investing, Licensing, and Trading Conditions Abroad*, October 1975, p. 20.

cast doubt on the longevity of PRI rule. The government is a major employer in Mexico, but it is under IMF pressure to reduce inflation drastically. It must, therefore, avoid public investments, such as expanding Mexico's steel industry, that could create significant numbers of new jobs in the country's centralized economy. Moreover, foreign investments have slowed down. Nevertheless, the PRI will be increasingly hard-pressed to muster public support if Mexico's growing labor force is not accommodated in the job market. As one Mexico-watcher concludes:

> With an inflation rate of more than 20 percent and underemployment estimated as high as 40 percent, this nation . . ., even the most optimistic observers agree, has a long and hard row to hoe.[173]

---

[173] Mullaney, "Optimism and Hope on Outlook in Mexico," p. D-11.

CHAPTER IV

The Mexican Labor Sector

Publications extolling Mexico's business climate frequently cite the country's excellent record of political stability, its vast natural resources, its large demographic market, and—until recently—its formidable economic growth. Rarely is Mexico's labor sector given more than cursory mention. Perhaps more than any other factor, however, the traditionally close relationship between government and labor in Mexico is the mainstay of the country's economic progress and stable political system. In this section, Mexico's little understood labor sector is reviewed in some detail to depict labor's vital role in Mexican politics and economics. Mexican labor, it will be shown, is becoming an unbridled force, and its demands and militancy now cast serious doubt on Mexico's economic and political future.

MEXICO'S LABOR LEGISLATION

Mexico's basic labor norms are set forth in the Constitution of 1917 and a host of subsequent federal decrees. Specifically, Article 123 of Mexico's constitution elaborates the rights and obligations of employers and employees in considerable detail. These constitutional provisions reflect the prestige which labor attained in the wake of the Mexican Revolution. As one Mexican businessman put it:

> Mexico's organized labor movement, like that of England and France, was an integral part of a revolution. In our country, it did not get into full swing until the first decade of the 20th century and it became part of a sweeping movement for basic economic, social and political changes. Up to that time, Mexico had the characteristics of a feudal state. Our population was divided rather sharply into a small aristocracy . . . and . . . the great majority of the population with a low standard of living.

Under such conditions, it was not surprising that our Constitution of 1917, product of the revolution of 1910, incorporated under Article 123 an extensive set of rules to protect the workmen. It was the first constitution in the world to include a Bill of Rights for the workmen, and at such time was considered to be quite radical.[1]

Two other articles of the Constitution of 1917 are also labor oriented. Article 4 guarantees workers the right to engage in any profession. Article 5 declares that no worker can be forced to work against his or her will nor be coerced to work without just compensation.

A series of federal labor decrees have complemented these constitutional provisions. The major laws which have modified or added to constitutional labor law in Mexico are cited in Table IV-1. It is significant that six of these thirteen key additions were promulgated after 1970 during President Echeverría's exceptionally prolabor mandate. This fact underscores the most important of the three main characteristics of Mexican labor law.

First of all, Mexican labor law is markedly prolabor. The labor norms established in the Constitution of 1917 are, in the words of one Mexican law book, "labor protective and defensive." [2] Subsequent federal decrees have accentuated this strongly prolabor tone. For example, current labor law requires employers in rural areas to provide (upon request) an unoccupied room which workers can use as a union office. According to one legislative survey, moreover:

> federal labor law is clearly intended to favor the employee in all relations with an employer and the law now contains the principle, previously sustained by the labor authorities and the Supreme Court, that in the case of doubt in the interpretation of the law, the most favorable treatment to the employee will always take precedence.[3]

---

[1] Eduardo Prieto Lopez, "Labor and Management in Mexico," *Seminar on Doing Business in Modern Mexico* (Berkeley: University of California at Berkeley, 1967), p. 59.

[2] Alberto Trueba Urbina and Jorge Trueba Barrera, *Nueva Ley Federal del Trabajo Reformada* (Mexico: Editorial Porrua, S.A., 1976), p. xxiii.

[3] Price Waterhouse & Co., *Doing Business in Mexico* (New York: Price Waterhouse & Co., 1975), p. 51.

TABLE IV-1
Major Extensions of Constitutional Labor Legislation

Decree dated August 31, 1929 (published in *Diario Oficial* on September 6, 1929) on social security provisions in Mexico.

Decree dated October 18, 1933 (published in *Diario Oficial* on November 4, 1933) on worker participation.

Decree dated December 30, 1938 (published in *Diario Oficial* on December 31, 1938) on strike legality.

Decree dated November 5, 1942 (published in *Diario Oficial* on November 18, 1942) on state enforcement of labor law.

Decree dated October 21, 1960 (published in *Diario Oficial* on December 5, 1960) regrouping Mexico's labor norms.

Decree dated October 6, 1961 (published in *Diario Oficial* on November 27, 1961) on minimum wages.

Decree dated November 20, 1962 (published in *Diario Oficial* on November 21, 1962) instituting compulsory profit sharing.

Decree dated February 9, 1972 (published in *Diario Oficial* on February 14, 1972) on night-shift work.

Decree dated November 8, 1972 (published in *Diario Oficial* on November 20, 1972) on subsidized housing for workers.

Decree dated February 4, 1974 (published in *Diario Oficial* on February 6, 1974) on state and federal enforcement of labor law.

Decree dated October 7, 1974 (published in *Diario Oficial* on October 8, 1974) on government authority in the labor sector.

Decree dated December 27, 1974 (published in *Diario Oficial* on December 31, 1974) on the employment equality of women.

Decree dated May 1, 1975 (published in *Diario Oficial* on May 2, 1975) on profit sharing.

Source: Alberto Trueba Urbina and Jorge Trueba Barrera, *Nueva Ley Federal del Trabajo Reformada* (Mexico: Editorial Porrua, S.A., 1976), pp. 13-14.

A second notable characteristic of Mexican labor law is that it gives the federal government considerable authority over labor matters. The enforcement of labor law is technically an obligation of state governments in Mexico. Mexico's constitution, however, asserts the authority of the federal government over labor matters in the textile, electric, motion picture, rubber, sugar, mineral, mining, hydrocarbon, railway, petrochemical, and steel industries. Furthermore, it is estimated that some 40 percent of all Mexican industry is located in the federal district, an area over which the federal government has absolute jurisdiction.

Third, Mexican labor law itemizes the rights of workers in very great detail. The Constitution of 1917 is, itself, "extraordinary in the detail of the guarantee of rights to workers incorporated in it as a constitutional document." [4] Federal decrees have added to this fine detail. As a result, the current body of Mexico's labor legislation distinguishes between a broad number of employment categories—*patrones* (employers), *empleados de confianza* (confidential employees), *empleados* (minor supervisory and office workers), *obreros* (manual workers), *trabajadores de planta* (permanent employees), *trabajadores eventuales* (workers as yet on temporary payroll), etc.,—and carefully prescribes the rights of each. In this respect, there is virtually no margin for disputes over basic rights or minimum working conditions at the bargaining table. In Mexico, all labor rights and required working conditions are prescribed and defined by law.

Working Conditions

The basic working conditions prescribed by Mexican law are highlighted in Table IV-2. The legal norms on minimum employment conditions are quite extensive. Labor laws specify the maximum number of hours per day, per shift, and per week that men, women, and children can work. Of course, shorter hours can be agreed to through collective bargaining. The laws also set forth minimum vacation periods and bonuses, severance and indemnity pay, and disability compensation. Employers who violate these minimum norms are subject to fines ranging from 100 to 20,000 pesos (approximately US$5.00-$1,000), imprisonment, and other penalties.

Of Mexico's many employment requirements, three merit special note. First, the work force of each firm in Mexico must be 90 percent Mexican. Although the law permits all firms considerable flexibility in numbering foreign executives and technicians *vis-à-vis* this percentage, it is usually difficult for foreign nationals to acquire any entry visa which permits employment in the country. Many multinational firms have found that connections with the appropriate government authorities help to circumvent the legal barriers and extensive red tape which make the employment of foreigners problematic. Even then, the wives

---

[4] Frederic Meyers, *Party, Government and the Labour Movement in Mexico: Two Case Studies*, Institute of Industrial Relations Reprint No. 170 (Los Angeles: University of California at Los Angeles, 1967), p. 135.

TABLE IV-2
Working Conditions in Mexico

Hiring	Only persons over 14 years of age may be legally employed. Minors ages 14 to 16 require parental, union, and police permission for employment.
	Workers must receive the terms of their employment in writing; unless otherwise stipulated, employment is understood to be permanent.
	No job candidate can be refused employment on the basis of age or sex.
	Minimum 90 percent of any firm's employees must be Mexican nationals, although executives may be excluded from the computation of that percentage.
Hours	Maximum 8 hours (day work), 7 hours (night work) and 7½ hours (mixed shifts) per day for 48 hour total work week.
	Workers must receive one day of rest—normally on Sunday—for each 6 days on the job; workers are also entitled to at least one half-hour of rest each work day.
	The typical work schedule is 8½ hours per day Monday through Friday, 5½ hours on Saturday.
	Overtime may not exceed 3 hours a day and 9 hours a week.
Remuneration	Remuneration for weekly day of rest, civil holidays, and vacations is guaranteed.
	Minimum salaries by economic zone and basic occupation are fixed by minimum wage boards and government decree. Salaries above minimum are negotiable; salaries for workers performing the same tasks in one firm must be equal.
	Overtime is fixed at 100 percent over hourly rate. Double-time is also payable when laborers must work through their lunch period.
	A Christmas bonus equivalent to at least 15 days' wages and payable before December 20 is guaranteed all workers.
	Pay schedules are fixed by collective contracts but cannot exceed one week intervals for manual workers, 15 days for all other employees.
	Withholding wages as a fine or punishment is strictly forbidden. Wage deductions to repay employers for pay advances or debts cannot exceed 30 percent of a worker's wages in excess of the minimum wage.

TABLE IV-2—Continued

Vacations and Holidays	Workers are guaranteed 7 legal holidays with pay each year: January 1 (New Year's Day), February 5, March 21 (Benito Juarez's birthday), May 1 (May Day), September 16 (Independence Day), November 20 (day commemorating Revolution of 1910), and December 25 (Christmas).
	December 1 (Presidential inauguration) is also a legal holiday each 6 years.
	Workers with one year's seniority are entitled to a paid vacation equivalent to at least 6 continuous workdays. Minimum vacation periods increase 2 days for each additional year's seniority up to 4 years' seniority; after 4 years, they increase 2 days for each 5 years' seniority.
	All workers are entitled to a vacation bonus equivalent to at least 25 percent of their vacation pay.
Special Features	Employers must provide preventive medicines to workers in areas where tropical and/or contagious diseases are prevalent.
	All firms must provide workers with "hygienic, comfortable housing" via contributions to a National Workers' Housing Fund.
	Employees are entitled to share in the profits of their firms in percentage amounts determined by the National Commission of Worker Profit Sharing.
	Workers disabled on the job are entitled to disability compensation from their employer at rates prescribed for each infirmity by Article 514 of the current labor law.
Women/Minors	Minors under 14 years of age may not be employed.
	Minors between the ages of 14 and 16 may work a maximum 6 hours per day in shifts permitting school attendance. No minor can work overtime, Sundays, or legal holidays.
	Persons under 16 are entitled to at least 18 workdays of paid vacation.
	Overtime and industrial nightwork (or work after 10 p.m. in commercial establishments) are prohibited for women.
	Maternity leave must be granted to pregnant employees 6 weeks prior to probable delivery and 6 weeks after.
	Working women nursing infants receive 2½ hour rest periods with full pay.

TABLE IV-2—Continued

Dismissals	Employment is temporarily suspended without pay when workers contact contagious diseases or are imprisoned, hospitalized for illnesses not work-related, or appointed to government posts.
	Employees can only be dismissed after written notice is served; dismissals for just cause do not require severance pay.
	"Just cause" dismissals require proof of industrial spying, flagrant dishonesty, lewd conduct on business premises, insubordination, unjustified absence of 3 or more days out of 30, drunkenness or criminal conviction.
	Employees with 20 or more years of seniority can only be dismissed for "extremely grave motives making continued employment impossible."
	Employees dismissed without just cause are entitled to 30 days' severance pay for each year of seniority and indemnity pay equivalent to 3 months' wages.
	Dismissal grievances can be taken before a Conciliation and Arbitration Board if workers so elect; unless proof of just cause is presented to the Board, employers may be required to reinstate dismissed workers with back pay and indemnity equivalent to 3 months' wages.

Sources: Alberto Trueba Urbina and Jorge Trueba Barrera, *Nueva Ley Federal del Trabajo Reformada* (Mexico: Editorial Porrua, S.A., 1976) ; U.S. Department of Labor, *Labor Law and Practice in Mexico*, BLS Report No. 240 (Washington: U.S. Government Printing Office, 1963).

of foreign executives are seldom permitted work visas if their husbands are allowed to work.

Second, overtime is legally restricted in Mexico to a maximum three hours per day and nine hours per week. Minimum overtime pay is 100 percent over the normal hourly rate. While this minimum is rather high by Latin American standards, collective contracts typically stipulate even higher overtime rates in individual firms.

Third, Mexican law requires that a Christmas bonus, equivalent to at least fifteen days' wages, and a vacation bonus, equivalent to at least 25 percent of vacation pay, be given to each worker. These minimum bonuses also tend to be adjusted higher in collective contracts. In many industries, they augment worker incomes considerably.

Profit Sharing

Since 1963, most concerns in Mexico—corporations, partnerships, or proprietorships—have been obliged by law to distribute a portion of their annual profits among their employees. Only newly established firms, mining firms still in the exploration phase, welfare institutions, and low capital firms given permission by the Ministry of Industry and Commerce are exempt from the profit-sharing requirement. In all other concerns, employees other than company directors and general managers are entitled to share in corporate profits. The actual amount of their collective share is set by a tripartite National Committee on Profit Sharing. At the present time, this amount stands at 8 percent of taxable corporate income.

It is significant that a 1975 amendment to Mexico's labor legislation revamped the basis for computing "sharable profits" and established federal norms for corporate compliance with the profit-sharing obligation.[5] The new law, together with Mexico's tax laws, defines profits or taxable income in a broad way, excluding only pension fund earnings, dividends received from Mexican companies, and certain gains from the exchange or sale of corporate securities. Eight percent of all other income is the total that must be shared with employees.

Specifically, the 8 percent portion of taxable profits is divided and then distributed in two equal parts. Fifty percent of this 8 percent lump sum is distributed among employees on the basis of the number of working days of each during the year. The remaining 50 percent is distributed according to the salaries earned by each. Boards composed of an equal number of management and labor representatives determine the specific profit share of each worker. Any dispute at the board level is referred to the area labor inspector. The final amounts determined by the boards (or inspectors) must be posted at each establishment and subsequently paid to employees no later than sixty days after the date on which annual income tax is due. Workers who object in any way to their allotments can submit a claim to Mexico's income tax authorities for federal review. Seldom, however, is this grievance procedure exercised or redress warranted.

Thus, profit sharing is a long and well-established practice in

---

[5] *Regulations made under sections 121 and 122 of the Federal Labour Act*, dated 1 May 1975 (*Diario Oficial*, 2 May 1975, No. 1, p. 24), cited in International Labour Office, "Mexico 1," *Legislative Series, 1975* (Geneva: ILO, 1977), pp. 1-6.

Mexico. Fines enforcing corporate compliance make *de facto* profit sharing commonplace. Even so, the right to share in corporate profits does not entitle workers to intervene in any way in the administration of their companies. Profit sharing often increases worker incomes by substantial amounts; but in Mexico's economy, this extra income adds to the country's inflationary propensity. In fact, local businessmen report that "profit-sharing has created for a large sector of the population a new source of income that is received in a lump sum, which has stimulated the market for durable goods, appliances, automobiles, homes, etc." [6] Although it is one of the highly sophisticated aspects of labor relations in Mexico, then, profit sharing is somewhat problematic *vis-à-vis* federal efforts to control inflation.

Social Security

Mexico's social security system is also an institution of long standing. It was first called for by the Constitution of 1917 and began full-scale operations in 1942. Today, social security benefits are extended to many Mexican workers via the Mexican Social Security Institute (*Instituto Mexicano de Seguro Social—IMSS*) which covers employees in the private sector. A separate but similar system, the Institute of Social Security and Services for Government Employees (*Instituto de Seguridad y Servicios Sociales de los Trabajadores del Estado*—ISSSTE), provides basically the same coverage for employees in the public sector. According to the current social security legislation, the aim of these institutes is to "guarantee the human right to health, medical assistance, . . . minimum living standards and the social services necessary for individual and collective well-being." [7] Although Mexico's social security programs are designed to protect workers against all social hazards, this welfare coverage is somewhat limited in practice.

Mexico's social security benefits are highlighted in Table IV-3. In the private sector, the IMSS provides modest disability and old age pensions, complete medical services, and very limited unemployment compensation to many industrial employees and their dependents. Under Mexican law, these benefits are available to all insured personnel, their legal or common-law wives, and their dependent parents and children under sixteen years

---

[6] Lopez, "Labor and Management," pp. 63-64.

[7] Instituto Mexicano del Seguro Social, *Ley del Seguro Social*, TITULO 1, ARTICULO 2 (1975).

TABLE IV-3
Social Security Benefits in Mexico

Sickness	After 4 days' waiting period, weekly payment is made by the IMSS corresponding to 54-60 percent of daily wages according to nine wage classes.
	This benefit is payable for a normal maximum of 52 weeks but may be extended an additional 26 weeks.
Injury and Disability	Employees temporarily disabled due to work-related injuries receive 100 percent of earnings according to nine wage classes. Benefits are payable from first day of incapacity until work is resumed or until permanent disability is declared.
	Permanently disabled workers receive monthly pensions, based also on wage class, ranging from 1,080 pesos to 70 percent of monthly earnings. They may additionally receive an annual bonus equivalent to one-half of one month's pension if the IMSS so authorizes.
	If a work injury results in death, two months' wages are paid to the insured's survivors in addition to normal death benefits.
Health Care	Full medical services—general and specialist care, surgery, hospitalization, dental care, medicines, and laboratory services—are provided to IMSS participants and their dependents.
Maternity	Working wives receive time off with full salary 42 days before and after the delivery of a child (total: 84 days).
	An allowance equivalent to 25 percent of earnings is payable to nursing mothers for up to six months after delivery.
	Medical services and layettes are provided by IMSS health facilities.
Old Age	Participants over 65 years of age are entitled to 35-45 percent of average earnings during the last 250 weekly contributions according to nine classes.
	Increments of 1.25-1.50 percent of earnings per year are payable to participants with more than 500 weekly contributions. An additional 2 percent increment is payable per year of work after age 65.
	Employees between the ages of 60 and 64 may retire with reduced pensions ranging from 75-95 percent of the full pension otherwise appropriate.
	Wives receive a 15 percent supplement—and each child under 16 (or 25 if a student or invalid) a 10 percent supplement—of a participant's old age pension.

TABLE IV-3—Continued

Death	A funeral grant equivalent to one month's earnings is paid if the insured made minimum twelve weekly IMSS contributions and received either an old age or disability pension. A two-month survivors' grant is paid if death results from work injuries.
	Widows are entitled to a pension equivalent to 50 percent of the old age or disability pensions—or 40 percent of the work injury pension—payable to an IMSS participant.
	Surviving children up to age 16, or 25 if a student or invalid, or dependent parents receive 20 percent of a deceased participant's pension(s).
Unemployment	No benefits are paid for unemployment unless related to sickness or disability.
Other Features	Workers who qualify for two or more pensions may not receive total payments in excess of 100 percent of the highest wage category. Widows or dependents who qualify for two or more survivors pensions may not receive total payments in excess of the maximum of any one pension.
	All benefits require minimum IMSS contributions ranging from 4 to 150 weekly quota payments.
	A marriage grant equivalent to 25 percent of the annual disability pension (up to maximum 6,000 pesos) is payable to participants.

Source: Instituto Mexicano del Seguro Social, *Ley del Seguro Social.*

of age (twenty-five if full-time students or invalids). In Mexico, employees are divided into nine wage groups for the purpose of computing social security benefits and premiums, and the pensions and benefits paid by the IMSS to these beneficiaries are specifically based on these nine wage categories. These categories now range from Group M, for those workers earning up to 50 pesos (approximately US$1.73) a day, to Group W, for those earning 280 pesos (US$9.70) or more a day.

What is particularly noteworthy is the actual scope of Mexico's social security coverage. The number of beneficiaries in the IMSS and the ISSSTE jumped some 27 percent between 1970 and 1974, increasing by 16.7 million people. Even so, the extension of social security coverage to rural areas in Mexico has been extremely problematic. Historically, few agricultural workers or their employers—overall, roughly 40 percent of Mexico's labor force—have been brought into the country's social security system. As a result, a revised social security law was promulgated in 1973 to include mandatorily all organized farm-workers in the IMSS. The law broadly defines an "organized worker" as any rural worker who at least belongs to a local farm cooperative if not a larger agricultural union. The definition was taken by many Mexican businessmen as further evidence of the government's reliance on organized labor to accomplish its social and economic goals.

In addition to the concentration of its coverage in the industrial and public sectors, two other features of Mexico's social security programs should be mentioned. First, unemployment compensation under the Mexican system is limited in cases of temporary illness, occupational disease, maternity, or job accidents. Unless a worker qualifies for compensation in these select instances, he or she is not given welfare income between jobs. Thus, most workers are economically forced to find work of some sort for day-to-day subsistence. This fact tends to accentuate underemployment—not unemployment—as a critical problem in Mexico.

Second, social security coverage is largely financed by employers in the private sector. Coverage for occupational injuries is financed entirely by employers at rates reflecting the statistically measured risk of each industry, while most other social security benefits are financed jointly by workers, the government, and employers, who pay the lion's share. Furthermore, many firms voluntarily pay their workers quotas or provide complementary pensions and medical services as fringe benefits. Details of the social security system's cost to employers are discussed in a subsequent section in this chapter.

Thus, Mexico's social security system provides diverse benefits to many Mexican workers, and the social security legislation has resulted in the construction of new hospitals, clinics, and, in some cases, schools for workers and their dependents. The coverage provided by Mexican social security is limited, however. Although the legislation now includes agricultural workers, most are not as yet included in the benefit scheme. Additionally, employers frequently provide extra pensions and dependent allotments to workers who are Institute participants to supplement available social security coverage.

Housing and Other Welfare Services

Aside from the fringe benefits they may provide voluntarily, employers are required to finance certain welfare services which are technically outside of Mexico's social security system. For example, concerns employing between 100 and 300 workers must maintain professionally staffed first-aid stations on their premises. Firms with more than 300 employees must provide hospital or clinic facilities as well. In addition, those firms located outside urban areas are required to provide schooling, water, and light service for workers and their families. Rural employers operating work centers five kilometers or more from any town must also provide tracts of land for a public marketplace, a municipal services' building, and a recreation center if the area's population exceeds 200. If any firm employs more than 400 workers, it must provide scholarships for workers and their dependents as well.

Of all the welfare services furnished exclusively by employers, however, housing is undoubtedly the major benefit called for by Mexican law. Mexico's government worked throughout the 1960s to force the business community to shoulder workers' housing costs and to undertake construction projects. According to one report, "Government pressure was increasing, but there was also an increased awareness that good housing would contribute to political stability and good labor relations." [8] Again, the rationale was that government-prompted (but corporate-financed) housing projects would generate more labor support to help perpetuate PRI rule.

Rural employers—again, those maintaining work centers outside the urban areas—must now provide comfortable housing for their workers, charging them no more than 0.5 percent of the property's appraised value for monthly rent. All employers, urban and rural alike, are further required to contribute 5 percent of their ordinary total payroll disbursements to the National Workers' Housing Fund Institute (*Instituto del Fondo Nacional de la Vivienda para los Trabajadores*—INFONAVIT), whether they provide residential quarters or not. Created in 1972, INFONAVIT finances housing construction and home mortgages for the Mexican worker. The Fund, managed by the government, was designed to help construct about 100,000 low-cost hous-

---

[8] Thomas E. Weil *et al.*, *Area Handbook for Mexico*, 2nd ed. (Washington, D.C.: U.S. Government Printing Office, 1975), p. 172.

ing units per year. Between 1972 and mid-1974, however, only 20,000 units were completed. As a result, on the one hand, some workers have become resentful of the Fund's "slow progress." On the other hand, because earlier legislation passed in 1970 had initially required employers to provide and finance wholly adequate housing for their workers by 1973, employers are relieved to confront less financial responsibility under the INFONAVIT program. Like the scholarships, utilities, medical facilities, and other benefits required by law, the current housing tax increases labor costs—but not by as much as the previous housing obligation. One further financial benefit of the current program is that the employers' housing contributions are considered to be social welfare payments and are deductible from their income taxes.

EMPLOYER COSTS OF SOCIAL WELFARE IN MEXICO

In Mexico, social security premiums are paid by the government, by employees according to one of the nine wage categories (M to W), and by employers.[9] Social security premiums are computed on the total earnings of each employee, excluding overtime pay, up to a maximum of ten times the minimum wage in Mexico City. Employer premiums amount to 9.375 percent of the median salary of Groups M to U and 9.375 percent of the actual earnings of the highest wage group, Group W, up to the tenfold minimum wage limit. For IMSS medical expenses and old-age pensions, excluding workmen's compensation, 12.5 percent of the total premium is contributed by the federal government, 25 percent is deducted from employee salaries, and 62.5 percent is paid by employers. The premium for occupational risks is paid exclusively by employers. It is computed as a percentage of total employee and employer contributions for old-age benefits and medical services. This "risk percentage" varies according to the risk class of each company, as indicated in Table IV-4. In practice, the employer cost of risk coverage typically ranges from 6 to 10 percent of a firm's total payroll.

Thus, the total cost of social welfare in Mexico varies according to a firm's location and risk class, the number of its employees, and the volume of their wages. Concerns located

---

[9] Information on employer social security costs was taken from Price Waterhouse & Co., *Doing Business in Mexico*, pp. 58-59. Readers desiring more detail on corporate obligations under Mexico's social security system may refer to that study.

TABLE IV-4
Premium Classes for Occupational Risk Coverage

Group		Average Additional Percentages
I	Commerce, the professions, administrative or sales offices (see below)	5
II	Some commerce, warehouses, very light manufacturing, laboratories	15
III	Light manufacturing, textiles, etc.	40
IV	High risk industry, using metals, chemicals, heat	75
V	Maximum risk, including construction, mining, heavy industry	125

Source: Commercial Office of the Mexican Embassy, Washington, D.C.

in rural areas may pay lower wages because of lower minimum wage standards. In addition to making the required social security contributions, however, rural employers must provide housing, utilities, and schooling to workers and their dependents. Regardless of location, all employers must pay Christmas and vacation bonuses (fifteen days' wages and 25 percent of vacation pay, respectively), contribute 8 percent of their taxable profits, pay workers for a weekly day of rest and civil holidays, deposit an amount equivalent to 5 percent of their total payrolls in the National Housing Fund, contribute towards IMSS old-age and medical benefits, and finance occupational risk coverage. The total fringe benefit cost, including profit sharing, adds "about 60% to base payroll expenses, depending on the salary level of the employee." [10] Nevertheless, overall labor costs are much lower in Mexico than in the United States. Some surveys, in fact, have estimated Mexico's labor cost to be about 50 percent lower than that of the United States.[11] This difference, however, is considerably offset by the lower productivity of Mexico's workers. As one United States government report recently noted, "Managers of industrial plants in Mexico often state that, because

[10] Business International Corp., "Mexico," *Investing, Licensing & Trading Conditions Abroad*, March 1977, p. 24.

[11] Lopez, "Labor and Management," p. 65.

of lower productivity, labor costs per unit of output are higher than would at first be indicated by daily wage levels." [12]

MEXICAN LABOR ORGANIZATIONS

Workers in Mexico enjoy freedom of association, and Mexico's constitution and labor laws specifically authorize the formation of labor organizations and define them by type. The Constitution of 1917 recognized the right of both workers and employers to form associations in defense of their interests. Mexico's Reformed Labor Law, now in effect, stipulates that twenty or more individuals may form a union for interest purposes. The law provides for plant unions (*de empresa*), craft unions (*gremiales*), industrial unions (*industriales*) formed by workers of more than one industrial concern, national industrial unions (*nacionales de industria*) formed by workers in the same industry employed in one or more interstate concern(s), intrastate or "regional" federations (*federaciones*), and labor confederations (*confederaciones*). Three million Mexican workers are organized which represents approximately 20 percent of the total work force; but if 49 percent of that work force is unemployed or underemployed, then Mexican labor is highly organized at 60 to 70 percent.[13]

Although unions cannot undertake commercial activities for profit, they have come to wield great economic and political power; and although no one may be legally forced to join or not to join a labor group, unions do have the right to require employers to discharge members who are expelled or resign from a union, if there is an exclusion clause in a collective contract. Each May Day, hundreds of thousands of union members stage a mass solidarity demonstration in Mexico City's main square led by labor leaders, who are themselves political chiefs, linking arms with the president of the republic. The spectacle is an awesome picture of the prominence that organized labor has attained in Mexico.

In the sections which follow, the historical evolution of Mexico's labor organizations is briefly reviewed; the main groups representing Mexican workers at this time are highlighted; and the growth and extent of Mexican trade union power are analyzed.

---

[12] U.S. Department of Commerce, *Establishing a Business in Mexico*, OBR 72-027 (Washington, D.C.: U.S. Government Printing Office, 1972), p. 13.

[13] Arthur B. Nixon, Labor Attaché, interview held at the United States Embassy, Mexico City, August 24, 1977.

Historical Overview

Mexican labor organizations have passed through three phases: mutualism, anarchosyndicalism, and trade-unionism. Labor organizations date back to the early 1800s in Mexico when artisans first formed mutual benefit societies. Not infrequently, these groups struck for better wages and demanded improved working conditions. By the latter part of the nineteenth century, however, the anarchist philosophy of Mikhail Bakunin and the Marxist, utopian-socialist schools of thought found fertile ground in Mexico. Worker cooperatives were formed throughout the country and labor groups became politically active in an attempt to establish a "workers' republic." [14] As a result, several administrations sought to squelch the political opposition which Mexico's syndicalist labor groups were fomenting. A civil code, promulgated in 1872, forbade all strikes and "worker conspiracies." After 1876, strikes and other labor activities were ruthlessly suppressed under Porfirio Diaz.

Despite their vicious repression, however, unions gained prestige and grew under the Diaz government. In fact, it was the discontent catalyzed by labor against the Diaz regime which helped touch off Mexico's Revolution in 1910 (see chapter II). A powerful labor group, the *Casa del Obrero Mundial,* "The Home of the World Worker," was established during the revolutionary period. It began aggressively organizing Mexican workers into trade unions and strongly supported the country's various revolutionary leaders. "Red Battalions"—worker armies organized by this group—fought on the side of Venustiano Carranza's revolutionary forces and contributed significantly to Carranza's military victory. This kind of collaboration with the revolutionary movement set the trend for organized labor's close rapport with postrevolutionary government and gave labor exalted status in postrevolutionary Mexico.

Today, trade unions are prevalent throughout Mexico with broad government support. Mexican labor law merely requires unions to register with the proper government authorities in order to function legally. Only bank employees and minors under 14 years of age are prohibited from becoming union members.

---

[14] Detailed information on the historical evolution of Mexican labor groups after 1860 is provided in Robert J. Alexander, *Organized Labor in Latin America* (New York: The Free Press, 1965), pp. 183-199. Readers seeking further background data are urged to consult that work.

The injunction against bank employee unions dates back to the Cárdenas administration in the 1930s:

> President Lázaro Cárdenas (1934-40) was prolabor and relied extensively on the labor movement for political backing. However, Cárdenas became convinced that the bank workers' union was becoming dominated by communists. . . . For this reason, he used a vague provision in the federal constitution to issue a decree in 1937 banning unionization of bank employees.[15]

Of course, the decree does provide certain benefits and labor standards for bank employees, even though they cannot unionize or engage in work stoppages. Indeed, the minimum wage for bank employees must be 50 percent higher than the local minimum wage; banks must provide their employees with extensive medical services; and the maximum banking work week is forty-two hours.[16]

In addition to their lack of members in the banking sector, Mexican labor organizations have other characteristics that are worthy of note. First, most labor groups have overlapping jurisdictions in Mexico. Mexican law has never regulated the structure of the labor movement so that no one labor group—whether organized on a craft, industrial, or geographic basis—has ever had a complete jurisdictional monopoly.[17] Second, most Mexican unions are affiliated with regional or national federations and confederations. We shall see, for example, that Mexico's largest labor group, the Mexican Workers' Confederation (CTM), incorporates no less than 59 to 70 percent of all union members. Third, as we have noted, Mexican unions generally operate in very close alliance with the country's dominant political party, the PRI. As one study observed:

> Most Mexican unions operate under the tutelage, if not the domination, of the PRI. Although union leaders formally participate in the Party's decisions, their primary function appears to be controlling the labor movement, while representing workers' interests in the Party is secondary.[18]

---

[15] Albert A. Blum and Mark Thompson, *Unions and White-Collar Workers in Mexico,* School of Labor and Industrial Relations Reprint Series No. 133 (East Lansing: Michigan State University, 1972), p. 655.

[16] *Ibid.,* p. 656.

[17] This trait of Mexican unions is discussed in Meyers, *Party, Government and the Labour Movement,* p. 137.

[18] Blum and Thompson, *Unions and White-Collar Workers,* p. 648.

Because of their close ties with the PRÏ, unions are "able to exert influence on the Government in varying degrees, while in return their backing gives the Government a basis of political stability." [19] Finally, most unions have considerable impact on the day-to-day work environment in Mexico; they negotiate collective agreements, enforce them, and present grievances and represent workers in Mexico's labor courts. In addition, they "control hiring through the operation of the closed shops which prevail in virtually all Mexican collective agreements." [20]

Management associations also exist; and, since the 1940s, firms capitalized at 500 pesos (approximately US$17) or more are legally obliged to join an official national chamber of commerce. These groups—such as the Confederation of Industrial Chambers (*Confederación de Cámaras Industriales*—CONCAMIN) and the Confederation of National Chambers of Commerce (*Confederación Nacional de Cámaras de Comercio*—CONCANACO)—have also cultivated close government ties. According to one United States government publication, "Although Mexico's semiofficial and private businessmen's organizations do not, as groups, actively participate in political elections, nearly every one of them has a close relationship with a corresponding organ of the Government." [21] Even so, these management groups have much less power than their labor counterparts.

Union Finances

Despite their political and economic strength, Mexican labor unions tend to be weak financially. Agricultural workers who are not extensively organized generally have such very low incomes that they rarely pay regular union dues. Industrial workers do contribute to their unions, but—if voluntary—their contributions are often skimpy. For this reason, "dues checkoffs," the deduction of union dues by employers from worker paychecks, are typically called for in collective contracts. Additionally, some unions derive some income from nondues sources.

Many firms are themselves required to contribute toward the support of independent or company unions in Mexico. For example, Clause 77 of the 1974-1976 collective contract nego-

---

[19] U.S. Department of Labor, *Labor Law and Practice in Mexico* (Washington, D.C.: U.S. Government Printing Office, 1963), p. 18.

[20] The examples of union power in Mexico were taken from Meyers, *Party, Government and the Labour Movement*, p. 143.

[21] U.S. Department of Labor, *Labor Law and Practice in Mexico*, p. 38.

tiated at Volkswagen's Mexican plant required that firm to pay 15,000 pesos a month (US$6,233 annually) to the plant union.[22] The contract also obliged Volkswagen to provide its workers with uniforms for the May Day solidarity demonstrations, an expense which directly enhanced the standing of the union as well. But even these kinds of employer outlays do not significantly complement union incomes. Some sources, therefore, have suggested that extensive government support and donations by religious groups have been necessary to sustain Mexico's many labor groups. It is not known to what extent such contributions actually do take place. In any event, many Mexican labor organizations are known to operate with very limited dues-generated incomes.

Union funds are subject to considerable scrutiny in Mexico. The current Reformed Labor Law requires union finances to be reviewed once every six months by membership assemblies. Labor unions are legally entitled to purchase buildings and furniture for their own use, but they cannot invest their funds in any commercial activities for the sake of profit. Unlike German unions, then, Mexican labor groups do not have commercial interests in the economy, but they do exercise considerable economic power in the form of wage demands, aggressive collective bargaining tactics, strike action, and, most recently, demands for strict price controls.

Major Labor Organizations

We have already indicated that labor organizations in Mexico serve political, as well as labor and economic, functions. The Institutional Revolutionary Party, the PRI, is comprised of three main sectors—agrarian, labor, and popular—as noted in chapter II. The popular sector is a catch-all body largely dominated by unions of government employees. These latter unions, however, are neither particularly aggressive nor demanding. According to one study published by Michigan State University, "unions of public employees concentrate on maintaining political support for the government."[23] The labor and agrarian sectors, however, are dominated by labor federations and confederations which are often quite demanding and politically oriented. When we speak of Mexico's main labor organizations, then we are pri-

---

[22] Sindicato Independiente de Volkswagen de Mexico S.A. de C.V., "Contrato Colectivo de Trabajo: 1974-1976," Planta Puebla, 1974, p. 34.

[23] Blum and Thompson, *Unions and White-Collar Workers*, p. 646.

marily referring to the country's large, blue-collar federations or confederations, which are closely allied with Mexico's ruling political party.

Provisions for the formation of labor federations and confederations are established by Mexico's constitution and labor laws. These groups have existed for many years and have come to wield considerable power in the country. Table IV-5 highlights the membership and leadership of Mexico's six main labor confederations. Of these, the Mexican Workers' Confederation (*Confederación de Trabajadores de México*—CTM) is unquestionably the most powerful.

The Mexican Workers' Confederation includes between 59 and 70 percent of all Mexican unionists in its membership. Since 1963, CTM membership has increased by an estimated 34 percent. Today, the organization claims 2,500,000 members, although a somewhat lower figure is probably more realistic. Its women's section, composed of workers' wives and women workers, is a frequently publicized element in Mexico's labor movement. But the most important feature of the CTM is the group's powerful, rather unique role in Mexico's government machinery. As one labor survey affirmed:

> the strongest labor union organization is the Confederacion de Trabajadores de Mexico (CTM), led for the past 30 years by Fidel Velazquez. It is a mainstay of the Institutional Revolutionary party (PRI) and is closely connected, but not subordinated, to the government. . . .[24]

With its push for higher wages, the CTM has charted an "increasingly autonomous path."[25] Nevertheless, the CTM is an integral part of the PRI and is the government party's semiofficial labor arm.

In Mexico, it is primarily the CTM which generates labor support for PRI government by maintaining the rank and file within the PRI fold. This function is critical and largely explains Mexico's steady record of single-party rule. In exchange for its labor support, the CTM enjoys considerable government patronage and is championed by the government as the preeminent voice of Mexican labor. The CTM places many of its members in key government positions. In fact, CTM leaders have held seats in the National Congress on a regular basis for more than

---

[24] Business International Corp., "Mexico," *Investing, Licensing, and Trading Conditions Abroad*, March 1977, p. 23.

[25] *Ibid.*, p. 21.

TABLE IV-5
Mexico's Major Labor Confederations

Name	Mexican Workers' Confederation (*Confederación de Trabajadores de México*—CTM).
Jurisdiction	Mexico's largest umbrella confederation covering aviation, cement, construction, electrical, farm, hotel, paper, petroleum, printing, and sugar workers.
Address	Confederación de Trabajadores de México Vallarta, No. 8 México, D.F. (Telephone: 546-42-18)
Claimed Members	2,500,000
Estimated Actual Membership	1,978,000
Local Affiliations	26 national unions, 29 state federations, 2 territorial federations, 1 federation in the federal district, and some 100 regional or municipal federations. Principal affiliates include the Federations of Workers of the States of Nuevo Leon (FTENL), Veracruz (FTEV), the Federal District (FTDF), and the Mexican Unions of Sugar Workers (STIASRM), Cement Workers (STICSRM), Electricians (SUTECRM), Petroleum Workers (STIQPCRM), and Telecommunications Workers (SNITRM).
Int'l Affiliations	Key organizer of Latin American Workers' Confederation (CTAL) in 1938, but withdrew in 1947. Affiliated with International Confederation of Free Trade Unions (ICFTU) since 1949, and with the ICFTU's Inter-American Regional Organization (ORIT) since 1953.
Leadership	Headed by Fidel Velázquez, secretary general since 1941. Velázquez is the most powerful labor spokesman in Mexico and politically second only to President López Portillo.
Observations	Organized in 1936. Is Mexico's most powerful labor organization, encompassing between 50 and 70 percent of all union members. Chief member of Labor Unity Bloc (BUO) and Labor Congress.

TABLE IV-5—Continued

Name	Federation of Civil Service Unions (*Federación de Sindicatos de Trabajadores al Servicio del Estado*—FSTSE).
Jurisdiction	All public sector employees except those in electrical power, petroleum, railroad, and social security activities.
Address	Federación de Sindicatos de Trabajadores al Servicio del Estado Antonio Caso, No. 35 México, D.F. (Telephone: 566-82-15)
Claimed Members	448,000
Estimated Actual Membership	416,000
Local Affiliations	Comprises 29 national unions in various government fields. Principal affiliates include the National Teachers' Union (SNTE) and the Communications and Transport Workers' Union (STCT).
Int'l Affiliations	The National Teachers' Union, a largely noncommunist FSTSE affiliate, is a member of the International Federation of Teachers' Trade Unions (member of the communist World Federation of Trade Unions).
Leadership	Leadership is strongly pro-government and is the base of the Institutional Revolutionary Party's "popular sector" support. Current secretary general is Daniel Espinosa Galindo.
Observations	Is second most influential confederation after CTM. Labor law requires FSTSE to remain independent from other union groups, although it is a member of the Labor Unity Bloc (BUO) and Labor Congress.

TABLE IV-5—Continued

Name	Regional Confederation of Mexican Workers (*Confederación Regional Obrera Mexicana*—CROM).
Jurisdiction	Membership is concentrated in the garment, shoe, textile, maritime, and port industries.
Address	Confederación Regional Obrera Mexicana Republica de Cuba, No. 60 México, D.F. (Telephone: 512-88-50)
Claimed Members	200,000
Estimated Actual Membership	142,700
Local Affiliations	1 confederation, 21 federations, and 193 trade unions.
Int'l Affiliations	Was Mexico's affiliate of ATLAS, the Peronist Latin-American labor organization, from 1952 to 1957.
Leadership	Historically, CROM officials have occupied important government posts. Current secretary general is Antonio J. Hernández.
Observations	Organized in 1918. Member of the Labor Unity Bloc (BUO), Labor Congress, and labor sector of the Institutional Revolutionary Party (PRI). Has extensively financed cooperatives, housing projects, schools and libraries throughout Mexico.

TABLE IV-5—Continued

Name	Revolutionary Confederation of Workers and Farmers (*Confederación Revolucionaria de Obreros y Campesinos* —CROC).
Jurisdiction	Membership primarily includes company unions in the textile, food, beverage, hospital, and transportation industries.
Address	Confederación Revolucionaria de Obreros y Campesinos San Juan de Letrán, No. 80-603 México, D.F. (Telephone: 512-69-91)
Claimed Members	164,000
Estimated Actual Membership	139,200
Local Affiliations	5 confederations, 44 federations, and 254 trade unions.
Int'l Affiliations	None.
Leadership	Presidency rotates annually between secretaries general of CROC's major confederation components. Current president is Manuel Rivera Anaya.
Observations	Formed in 1952 by merger of 4 small confederations to challenge the CTM's labor dominance. Is chief member of the National Workers' Center (CNT); also member of Labor Congress.

TABLE IV-5—Continued

Name	General Conference of Workers (*Confederación General de Trabajadores*—CGT).
Jurisdiction	Membership chiefly consists of construction and textile workers, bakers (Mexico City), bus drivers, and some farm workers.
Address	Confederación General de Trabajadores 5 de Febrero, No. 73 México, D.F. (Telephone: 521-63-08)
Claimed Members	36,000
Estimated Actual Membership	21,450
Local Affiliations	8 federations and 34 trade unions.
Int'l Affiliations	None.
Leadership	Current secretary general is Cecilio Salas Gálvez.
Observations	Formed in 1921. Membership concentrated in Mexico City, but influence and strength are weak. Member of Labor Unity Bloc (BUO) and Labor Congress.

TABLE IV-5—Continued

Name	Revolutionary Confederation of Workers (*Confederación Revolucionaria de Trabajadores*—CRT).
Jurisdiction	Membership broadly includes industrial and farm workers.
Address	Confederación Revolucionaria de Trabajadores Niño Perdido, No. 16-3er. piso México, D.F. (Telephone: 578-92-15)
Claimed Members	28,000
Estimated Actual Membership	11,800
Local Affiliations	None.
Int'l Affiliations	None.
Leadership	Secretary general is Mario Suárez.
Observations	Formed in 1954. Since its organization, two splinter groups separated from the CRT—the Federation of Labor Groups (FAO) and the Revolutionary Workers' Federation (FRT)—to form the Revolutionary Labor Federation (FOR).

Source: The data presented in Table IV-5 are synthesized from confidential sources.

thirty years. The Confederation has a strong—and according to some analysts, the dominant—voice in the selection of the PRI's candidate for president, Mexico's presidential heir apparent, every six years. It controls eight votes in the General Assembly of the National Workers' Housing Fund; it exerts very strong influence on Mexico's Minimum Wage Boards and Labor Courts; and its presence is felt in virtually every federal ministry, every state and municipal government office, and most industrial plants.

In recent years, the CTM has campaigned vigorously for two major reforms. One is a reduction of the work week from forty-eight to forty hours. Until this change is incorporated in the body of Mexico's labor laws, the CTM has urged its affiliates to press for a reduced work week at the bargaining table. More recently, the CTM has demanded reforms in Mexico's federal labor laws so that escalator clauses can be officially incorporated in labor contracts. The government's reaction to these demands, however, are especially significant. According to one 1976 economic study:

> The labour minister, Sr. Gálvez Betancourt, far from dismissing out of hand the suggestion of an indexed wage system, made an official note of the CTM resolutions but warned that priority would have to be given to tackling the problem of rising prices. The employers were not so calm about the indexation suggestion. . . . They feel that indexation would take the responsibility of wage negotiations still more out of the employers' hands and give them even less control over wage costs movements.[26]

Because the government is increasingly concerned with the growth of splinter labor groups in Mexico and with the CTM's weakening grip on the country's labor sector, both of the CTM's current demands will most probably be implemented. It was pointed out earlier in this study that the CTM is beginning to lose control over Mexico's rank and file. Inflation and the 10 percent wage increase ceiling in effect from December 1976 to August 1977 seriously tarnished the CTM's reputation as labor's tough bargaining agent. Indeed, some analysts have insisted that organized labor's support is so vital to the PRI that the government would have to make some type of wage concession. In the words of *The Economist*:

---

[26] *Mexico*, Economist Intelligence Unit Quarterly Economic Review No. 2 (London: EIU, 1976), p. 3.

The government retains basic control over the Mexican workers' Confederation (CTM), which is one of three sectors of the ruling Institutional Revolutionary Party. But, in face of the growth of "independent" and frequently left-wing unions, the government must also retain the credibility of the godfather-like Don Fidel [Velázquez] and other CTM leaders. Given the choice of having to crush strikes led by independent unions or settling with the CTM at rates higher than 10%, the administration may therefore soon be forced to opt for the latter.[27]

Even if the rank and file's complaints are federally resolved, other CTM problems loom on the immediate horizon. CTM leadership will unquestionably be a critical concern in the not too distant future. Fidel Velázquez, reputed to be the second most powerful man in Mexico after the president of the republic, has ruled over the CTM without interruption since 1941. In 1962, he was unanimously reelected by the National Congress to his fourth 6-year term as the CTM's secretary general, and shortly thereafter "the National Congress changed the CTM's constitution to provide that no officer may succeed himself in any elected position in the future." [28] That restriction was never upheld, however; and 78-year-old Velázquez continues to rule the CTM with an iron hand. Furthermore, Velázquez has not yet designated nor begun to groom any successor to take his place. The secretary general's retirement or leave of absence for health reasons is therefore likely to leave the CTM with a critical leadership problem. Without Velázquez, the continued prominence of the CTM will surely be subject to question.

Second in size and influence to the CTM is the Federation of Civil Service Unions (*Federación de Sindicatos de Trabajadores al Servicio del Estado*—FSTSE). It is technically independent of all other labor groups and includes most public employees. As one report noted, "A special statute encourages civil servants to organize but prohibits them from joining confederations which include workers from the private sector." [29] Even so, the FSTSE does take part in Mexico's labor hierarchies. The FSTSE serves a dual function: it is one of the mainstays of the PRI's so-called popular sector, generating the support of Mexico's civil servants for PRI rule and providing much of the manpower for the Party's machinery; it also negotiates working conditions and wages for the public sector with top-level govern-

---

[27] "No El Dorado," *The Economist*, April 9, 1977, p. 85.

[28] U.S. Department of Labor, *Labor Law and Practice in Mexico*, p. 34.

[29] Blum and Thompson, *Unions and White-Collar Workers*, p. 648.

ment officials. Since PRI membership and support are prerequisites for most key civil service posts, however, the FSTSE is not particularly demanding.

Other labor groups which merit special mention are the Regional Confederation of Mexican Workers (*Confederación Regional Obrera Mexicana*—CROM) and the Revolutionary Confederation of Workers and Farmers (*Confederación Revolucionaria de Obreros y Campesinos*—CROC). First established in 1918, the CROM is Mexico's oldest labor confederation. Its formation was the product of Mexican anarchosyndicalism; and for many years, the CROM was extremely active in the country. By 1927, for example, it had organized more than 1,000 strikes representing the loss of more than 2 million workdays.[30] The CROM is a comparatively weak organization at the present time, however, with affiliates largely concentrated in Puebla, Veracruz, Baja California, Colinia, and Mexico's port cities. It is also a member of the labor sector of the PRI, but it is best known for the housing projects and clinics which it has funded. The CROC, the Revolutionary Confederation of Workers and Farmers, is also a PRI affiliate, but it enjoys even less prestige in Mexico. Formed in 1952 to challenge the labor dominance of the CTM, the CROC has failed to make any headway toward that objective. Its membership is concentrated in Baja California, the State of Mexico, and the federal district. CROC membership figures and activities are wholly eclipsed by those of the much more powerful CTM.

In addition to these confederations, other confederations—such as the General Confederation of Workers (*Confederación General de Trabajadores*—CGT) and the Revolutionary Confederation of Workers (*Confederación Revolucionaria de Trabajadores*—CRT)—also figure among the most prominent of Mexico's labor groups. They claim even smaller memberships than that claimed by the CROC, and they are not particularly active. Even so, these major confederations and Mexico's more powerful trade unions are organized into important "labor blocs."

The attempt to centralize Mexico's many labor organizations has a lengthy history. Mexico's PRI governments have long encouraged attempts to create a single labor body which would keep all of Mexico's workers—in one businessman's words—"un-

---

[30] Salvador Hernandez, "La revolucion mexicana y el niovimiento obrero: 1900-1925," *Sumario*, Vol. XXVIII, No. 2 (October 1973), p. 41.

der Party wraps." [31] These efforts have met with only partial success. As one study noted some time ago:

> Although political factors tend to make the trade union movement somewhat monolithic, factional differences within the PRI as well as regional differences have had a divisive effect. In fact, the Mexican labor movement has never really been united. Frequent efforts to unify the bulk of the trade union movement into a single country-wide organization have been unsuccessful. Recently, however, the drive for unity has been strengthened partly because increased anti-Communist feeling has drawn trade union leaders together and partly because the PRI appears to favor unity. [32]

Today, three large "umbrella" organizations exist in Mexico, as depicted in Figure IV-1. All three give allegiance to the PRI, although two of the groups are themselves rivals.

The Labor Unity Bloc (*Bloque de Unidad Obrera*—BUO) is comprised of four of Mexico's six major confederations and almost all of the country's large, independent industrial unions. Created in 1949 at the initiative of the CTM, the BUO was the first fruit of Mexican labor's unification efforts. It was not able to encompass all labor groups, however, due to factional squabbles over voting and representational procedures. Even so, the BUO currently represents 80 to 85 percent of Mexico's labor movement. Of its many members, moreover, the BUO's most prominent and all-powerful affiliate is the CTM. An alternative group, the National Workers' Center (*Central Nacional de Trabajadores* —CNT) was formed in late 1960 to rival the BUO. The most influential CNT affiliate is the Revolutionary Confederation of Workers and Farmers (CROC), the group which was formed to challenge the CTM's predominance in the labor sector. CROC membership—currently estimated at 139,200—is greater than that of all other CNT affiliates combined, however; thus, the National Workers' Center is not a particularly powerful body. It also supports Mexico's ruling government body, but is genuinely dwarfed by the much more powerful and much larger Labor Unity Bloc (BUO).

Members of both the BUO and the CNT are also integrated in Mexico's largest labor bloc, the *Congreso del Trabajo* or Mexican "Labor Congress." Set up in 1966 under government

---

[31] Notes from author's conversation with Monterrey businessmen, April 15, 1977, Philadelphia, PA.

[32] Martha Lowenstern, *Foreign Labor Information—Labor in Mexico* (Washington, D.C.: U.S. Bureau of Labor Statistics, 1958), p. 5.

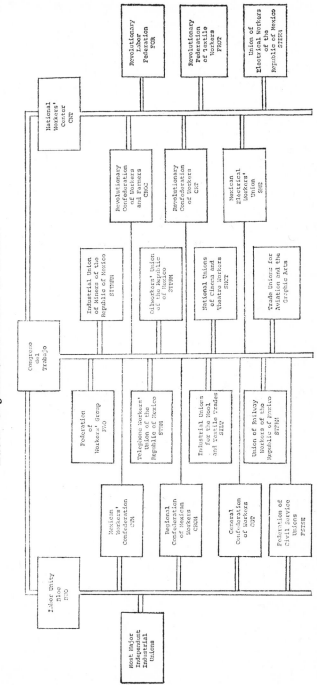

FIGURE IV-1
Labor Organization Blocs in Mexico

Source: Compiled from confidential sources.

auspices in yet another attempt to centralize all trade union organizations, the Labor Congress comprises more than thirty-one labor entities at this time. It represents most of Mexico's organized labor force—90 percent of the country's overall union membership—and can best be described as a 'loosely organized . . . council of "official" labor organizations.' [33] In other words, Mexico's Labor Congress unifies all major labor groups which have avowed allegiance to the PRI. The Congress is allegedly an independent labor center, but it functions under the shadow of the CTM, much like the Labor Unity Bloc. For example, the Labor Congress is technically headed by Armando Victoria Galván, the current Congress president, but Fidel Velázquez, secretary general of the CTM, is the *de facto* "power of the *Congreso.*" [34] In this respect, Mexico's two largest labor blocs are largely subordinate to the CTM.

There are, of course, worker organizations which operate outside the orbit of the Mexican Workers' Confederation and the Institutional Revolutionary Party. Three of these independent groups—the Independent Federation of Workers (*Federación Nacional de Sindicatos Independientes*—FNSI), the General Union of Workers and Farmers (*Unión General de Obreros y Campesinos de México*—UGOCM), and the Authentic Workers' Front (*Frente Auténtico del Trabajo*—FAT)—are noteworthy factions in Mexico's labor movement.

Many trade unions in the highly industrialized area around Monterrey are unique in that they are not affiliated with Mexico's national labor groups. Instead, these Monterrey unions are typically linked with the Independent Federation of Workers, the FNSI, which is one of the main organizations outside of Mexico's "official" labor family. The FNSI comprises 145,000 members—most of which are affiliates of company unions in the Monterrey area. [35] Although the FNSI does assist its members in presenting claims against management before Mexico's labor authorities, strikes organized by FNSI affiliates are quite rare. In fact, because of the FNSI's traditionally close rapport with management, FNSI members "generally receive higher pay, more

---

[33] Arthur B. Nixon, U.S. Labor Attaché to Mexico, to the author, February 23, 1977.

[34] *Ibid.*

[35] *Ibid.*

fringe benefits, and better working conditions than workers in unions associated with national federations." [36]

Several nonregional independent labor groups, which are generally not so cooperative, have also attained considerable notoriety. One such group, the General Union of Workers and Farmers of Mexico (UGOCM), primarily includes underemployed construction and agricultural workers and is well known for its labor agitation. Organized in 1949, the UGOCM is not a registered trade union organization per se and, therefore, has no collective bargaining rights. Even so, the UGOCM is rather active. It is the labor arm of the Popular Socialist Party (PPS) and was the known instigator of several peasant land invasions in Northern Mexico in the 1960s. In this sense, the UGOCM enjoys the not-exaggerated reputation of being an aggressive, militant labor group in Mexico. Its militancy is quite pale, however, in comparison with the extremely aggressive tactics of the Authentic Workers' Front, the FAT, which is undoubtedly the "hardest line" labor body in Mexico today.

The rise of the FAT in Mexico's labor movement is a critical signal of the loss of power now being felt by the country's traditional labor leadership. Founded in 1966 to challenge the CTM, the FAT has paradoxically fused together two rather antagonistic Mexican political philosophies. It has rallied Christian-Democratic unions with considerable religious support, on the one hand, and Marxist trade unions with sophisticated infiltration tactics on the other. Combining socialist ideology with extensive indoctrination and carefully planned demonstrations of militancy, the FAT is slowly gaining more and more blue-collar support, if not actual membership. At the present time, some fifty-three unions are known to be FAT affiliates, although a more precise membership breakdown for the group is not publicly available. What is clear, however, is that the FAT has stepped up its activities in Mexico. It is particularly active in the country's automobile plants—Dina Nacional (Renault), Nissan-Mexicana, and Volkswagen de México, to cite a few examples—and primarily directs its attacks against allegedly corrupt, CTM-affiliated labor leaders and multinational firms. This latter fact is perhaps best illustrated by the FAT's startling strike record in recent years.

Typically, the FAT agitates the rank and file at a multinational plant against "do-nothing" traditional union leaders, then

---

[36] U.S. Department of Labor, *Labor Law and Practice in Mexico*, pp. 35-36.

organizes a plant shutdown to boost its image as an activist labor entity. In recent years, the group has temporarily closed down the Majestic Electronics plant in Tlaxcala and Nissan's manufacturing facilities in Cuernavaca. According to a 1975 projected labor survey, moreover:

> because of a schism in the generally united labor front, some companies have had problems recently, Searle, General Electric and Spicer among them. In all three cases, management and CTM-affiliated union leaders had completed contract negotiations when representatives of a splinter group called the Frente Autentico del Trabajo (FAT) sponsored worker unrest by discrediting CTM leaders and claiming that the workers had been poorly represented at the bargaining table. In all three cases, this led to prolonged problems, although officially the negotiations had been completed and the new contracts were legal. GE finally dismissed members of the dissident group, with tacit government approval. Spicer did the same but eventually took them back after dissident leaders staged a prolonged hunger strike on the steps of the Labor Ministry.[37]

It is this kind of ploy which has captured considerable public attention as well as blue-collar support for the FAT.

To counter FAT gains, the CTM has mobilized (although somewhat slowly) to reaffirm its image as the paternalistic watchdog of Mexico's labor sector. Clearly, Fidel Velázquez' current drive for wage indexation is aimed at defending the CTM's dominant position in the labor movement against FAT attacks. Nevertheless, the FAT has already infiltrated a great number of plants and labor organizations. It now has a reasonably strong foothold in Mexico. According to one confidential document, "It can be said with some certainty that, in the labor sector, FAT has infiltrated all the central labor blocs and a large number of labor courts; in other sectors, this infiltration has been carried out by Christian-Democrat partisans." [38]

Understandably, the growth of the FAT is worrying businessmen and PRI politicians alike. From the management point of view, executives who work in Mexico affirm that FAT activists "try to gain adepts by attacking the business enterprises, and very specially [*sic*] multinationals," but they also point out that "their main attack is directed toward corrupt labor leaders, which

---

[37] Business International Corp., "Mexico," *Investing, Licensing, and Trading Conditions Abroad*, October 1975, p. 21.

[38] Confidential report on FAT activities and membership originally prepared for the management of a U.S. multinational firm in Mexico.

makes it most difficult to develop strategies and formulas to counterattack their arguments." [39]

Even though CTM leadership is the prime target of FAT belligerency, then, most multinational managers would rather negotiate with a traditional, nationally-directed labor group than have to deal with the FAT's militant representatives. From a political point of view, moreover, FAT activities in Mexico illustrate the contest already under way between the country's traditional, CTM-dominated, PRI-allied labor organizations and new, aggressive, and politically disrespectful splinter groups. Indeed, inflation, wage dissatisfaction, and radical splinter groups such as the FAT are beginning to sway the rank and file away from the CTM's sphere of influence.

International Affiliations

Mexican labor law makes no restriction on international labor affiliations. Because of this legal freedom and because of the country's earlier status as one of Latin America's foremost industrialized nations, Mexico has long been the seat of a number of transnational labor bodies. The headquarters of the Latin American Workers' Confederation (*Confederación de Trabajadores de America Latina*—CTAL) and the Inter-American Regional Organization of Workers (*Organización Regional Interamericana de Trabajadores*—ORIT) have been located in Mexico since 1938 and 1952, respectively. ORIT, the hemispheric arm of the International Confederation of Free Trade Unions (ICFTU), primarily has a following among Mexico's CTM-affiliated unions and has strived to bring the CTM into closer contact with United States unions on a number of mutual interest issues. Mexico's membership potential has attracted numerous other international labor representations as well. "For a considerable time," according to one United States government study, "Mexico City was the seat of a number of regional offices of International Trade Secretariats (ITS)." [40] It is significant, however, that this ITS presence in Mexico has slumped considerably in recent years.

Table IV-6 highlights the Mexican activities and memberships of the major international trade secretariats. It makes clear that few secretariats now operate in Mexico with notable commitment

---

[39] Author's correspondence with U.S. executives based in Mexico.

[40] U.S. Department of Labor, *Labor Law and Practice in Mexico*, p. 36.

TABLE IV-6

The International Trade Secretariats in Mexico

International Secretariat	Claimed Affiliate Membership	Activities in Mexico
International Federation of Building and Woodworkers (IFBWW)	Sindicatos Madereros dependientes de la Federación de Chihuahua (500) Sindicatos Madereros dependientes de la Federación de Durango (500) Sindicato de Trabajadores de la Industria del Cemento y Similares de la República Mexicana (membership not stated)	Representative in Argentina "takes care of all the unions . . . on this continent." However, IFBWW publications make no mention of any specific activities in Mexico.
International Federation of Chemical, Energy and General Workers (ICEF)	Sindicato de Trabajadores de la Industria del Cemento Cal, Yeso y sus Productos (15,000) Sindicato de Trabajadores de la Industria Química, Petroquímica, Carboquímica, Similares y Conexos de la República Mexicana (7,000)	ICEF's 1976 Activities Report states that "messages of support and solidarity," "protests to parent and/or local management," "public information campaigns," and "company data for use in collective bargaining" were provided Mexican workers in 1973. Research indicates that the extensiveness of these claims cannot be supported; rather, ICEF sent a few telegrams and letters of support to Mexican unions. Since 1973, no specific ICEF involvement has been reported.

TABLE IV-6—Continued

International Secretariat	Claimed Affiliate Membership	Activities in Mexico
International Federation of Commercial, Clerical and Technical Employees (FIET)	None in Mexico.	None in Mexico.
International Federation of Plantation, Agricultural and Allied Workers (IFPAAW)	Sindicato de Trabajadores de la Industria Azucarera y Similares de la República Mexicana (10,000)	Co-sponsored Latin American and Caribbean Sugar Workers' Conference in Mexico (1976) with IUF and Mexican affiliate. No other IFPAAW activities in the country are claimed.
International Graphic Federation (IGF)	None in Mexico.	None in Mexico.

TABLE IV-6—Continued

International Secretariat	Claimed Affiliate Membership	Activities in Mexico
International Metalworkers' Federation (IMF)	Consejo Nacional Obrero de las Industrias Eléctricas y Electrónicas (15,000)	Maintains regional office in Mexico City which produces the Spanish publication *Metal* several times annually.
	Consejo de la Industria Metal-Mecánica (10,000)	Organizes seminars for Ford, GM, Nissan, VAMSA (American Motors), General Electric, Union Carbide, and ITT workers in Mexico.
	Consejo Nacional Obrero de la Industria Automotriz de la República Mexicana (15,000)	Has organized National Auto Councils which provide training, collective bargaining and "solidarity" assistance to Mexican auto workers.
	Unions of Philips Workers, Radio Mercantile Workers, and Electronic Workers in Frontier Plants (memberships not stated)	Financial aid was provided during General Motors' strikes in 1973, 1975 & 1977.

TABLE IV-6—Continued

International Secretariat	Claimed Affiliate Membership	Activities in Mexico
International Transport Workers' Federation (ITF)	Asociación Sindical de Pilotos Aviadores (740) Unión Nacional de Marineros, Fogoneros, Mayordomos, Cocineros, Camareros y Similares del Golfo de México (250) Sindicato Nacional de Alijadores Empleados en Agencias Aduanales Marinos, Cargaduría y Similares (5,000) Sindicato de Trabajadores Ferrocarrileros de la República Mexicana (32,500) Sindicato de Empleados de Radio Aeronáutica Mexicana —SERAM (250) Sindicato Nacional de Trabajadores de Aviación y Similares—SNTAS (3,980) Asociación Sindical de Sobrecargos de Aviación de México (1,500) Sindicato Nacional de Técnicos y Trabajadores de Aeronaves de México (3,000)	Trade union education seminars are organized periodically. ITF Inter-American Conferences have been hosted by Mexican affiliates. Provided "solidarity assistance" to striking Mexican airline workers in 1976.

TABLE IV-6—Continued

International Secretariat	Claimed Affiliate Membership	Activities in Mexico
	Asociación Sindical Oficiales de Máquinas de la Marina Mercante Nacional (370)	
	Orden de Capitanes y Pilots **Navales** de la República Mexicana (755)	
	La Unión de Maquinistas Ayudantes y Mecánicos de Combustión Interna **del** Estado de Veracruz (120)	
	Unión de Estibadores y **Jornaleros** del Puerto Veracruz (285)	
	Sindicato Gremio Unido de Alijadores de Tampico y Ciudad Madero (**500**)	
International Union of Food and Allied Workers' Associations (IUF)	Sindicato de Trabajadores de la Industria Embotelladora de Aguas Gaseosas (10,000)	No "solidarity action" in Mexico from 1973-1976. However, local seminars and meetings on hotel and restaurant unionization were organized in 1970, 1971 and 1973.
	Sindicato Unico de Trabajadores **de** la Industria de la Carne (3,000)	
	Sindicato Industrial del Pan (**3,000**)	
	Sindicato Nestlé (1,200)	Co-sponsored 1976 Sugar Workers' Conference in Mexico with IFPAAW.
	Sindicato de los Trabajadores de **la** Industria Azucarera—STRIASM (20,000 "part-paying" **affiliates**)	

TABLE IV-6—Continued

International Secretariat	Claimed Affiliate Membership	Activities in Mexico
	Sindicato de Trabajadores de la Industria Hotelera, Gastronómica y Conexos de la República Mexicana (5,500) Unión Sindical de Trabajadores de las Industrias Dulcera, Repostera, Chocolatera y Conexos del Distrito Federal y Estado de México (membership not stated)	
Postal, Telegraph and Telephone International (PTTI)	Sindicato de Telefonistas de la República Mexicana—STRM (10,000)	Circulates comparative studies of working conditions throughout Latin America. Between 1969-1973, however, no seminars or trade union courses were sponsored in Mexico.

Sources: Complete references are cited in Appendix B.

or support. Only one international secretariat—the International Metalworkers' Federation (IMF)—maintains a regional office in the country at the present time.

The International Federation of Chemical, Energy and General Workers (ICEF) currently claims affiliation of 22,000 Mexican members, a 7,000 increase over the Mexican membership claimed in 1973.[41] Even so, there are no Mexican officers on any of the ICEF's various committees. Eleven members of the ICEF's latest (and second) Mexican affiliate, the *Sindicato de Trabajadores de la Industria Química, Petroquímica, Carboquímica Similares y Conexos,* did attend that secretariat's most recent world congress in 1976 in Montreal. Their reported contribution, however, was to co-sign a resolution calling for ICEF assistance to establish "free trade union association" in "Peru and in Latin America in general." [42] In 1973, the ICEF specifically called for the mobilization of its affiliates to unionize migrant foreign workers— "African workers in France, Turkish workers in Germany, Mexican illegal farm labourers in the US, etc."—whose "situations . . . are shocking, particularly in respect to housing, social and family amenities which are extensively deficient." [43] Yet the injunction—at least with regard to Mexico—was more an example of bravado rhetoric than it was of international labor solidarity. Indeed, it was highly improbable that the ICEF's United States affiliates would proselytize *illegal* Mexican workers for union membership in a decade when United States union officials were publicly demanding a crackdown on Mexican entries into the United States and insisting that "Mexican workers . . . in particular are stripping jobs away from American workers." [44]

The International Federation of Plantation, Agricultural and Allied Workers (IFPAAW) claims a single affiliate in Mexico, a Mexican sugar workers' union, although it had estimated in 1971

---

[41] ICF, *16th Statutory Congress, 27-29 October 1976, Montreal: Executive Committee; Activities Report of the Secretary General; List of Membership* (Geneva: ICF, 1976), p. 131; and "Affiliated Organizations, Votes," *ICF Bulletin,* 15th Congress Issue (1973), p. 143. Note: The ICF added the word *Energy* to its name and the initial *E* to its abbreviation at its 16th Statutory Congress. References in this study are to both the ICF and the ICEF.

[42] ICF, "Congress Documents," *16th Statutory Congress,* appended.

[43] "Report of Activities of the Secretary General," *ICF Bulletin,* 15th Congress Issue (1973), p. 116.

[44] James P. Sterba, "Cheap Mexican Labor Attracts U.S. Companies to the Border," *New York Times,* May 13, 1977, pp. A-1 and A-10.

that as much as 52 percent of Mexico's population was then engaged in agriculture.[45] The IFPAAW recently acknowledged that "the hoped for cooperation from this affiliate in assisting in organisational activities in other sectors in agriculture . . . has not materialised."[46] More precisely, the IFPAAW has made no headway in attracting more Mexican support, and its lone Mexican affiliate is known to have contributed only US$420 in dues between 1961 and 1971.[47]

Other secretariats have largely the same or an even poorer standing in the country. The Postal, Telegraph and Telephone International (PTTI) claims only one Mexican affiliate (10,000 members) at this time.[48] Interestingly enough, the CTM reportedly helped the PTTI to establish a regional office in Mexico City in the 1950s.[49] By 1974, however, the PTTI only maintained offices in Argentina, Ecuador, and Washington, D.C. The International Federation of Commercial, Clerical and Technical Employees (FIET) and the International Graphic Federation (IGF) claim no Mexican affiliates whatsoever. The International Transport Workers' Federation (ITF), which claims the greatest Mexican-affiliated membership of all the major secretariats, has lost a significantly large number of local partisans in the past seven years.

The ITF has regularly reported Mexican delegations at its international congresses and provides solidarity support—cables, correspondence, etc.,—to striking Mexican affiliates. Additionally, in 1976, the ITF-affiliated Canadian Air Line Flight Attendants' Association allegedly refused—"at the request of the ITF"—to operate routes otherwise manned by striking Mexican cabin attendants, themselves ITF affiliates.[50] Nevertheless the ITF's affiliated membership in Mexico has drastically declined. In 1970, the ITF claimed 101,173 dues-paying members in Mexico; by the

---

45 IFPAAW, "Regional Activities Report," *Report of the Secretariat, IFPAAW Third World Congress* (Geneva: IFPAAW, 1971), p. 42.

46 IFPAAW, "Regional Activities Report," *Fourth World Congress* (Geneva: IFPAAW, 1976), p. 31.

47 IFPAAW, "Current Position in Relation to Affiliations," *Report of the Secretariat, IFPAAW Third World Congress* (Geneva: IFPAAW, 1971), p. 5.

48 Departmento de Estudios e Informaciones Laborales, *La Internacional del Personal de Correos, Telegrafos y Telefonos en las Americas* (Washington, D.C.: PTTI, 1976), p. 44.

49 *Ibid.*, p. 13.

50 ITF, *XXXII Congress, Dublin, 21-29 July 1977: Report on Activities—1974-1975-1976* (London: ITF, 1977), p. 32.

outset of 1977, that number dropped by more than 50 percent to a much lower 49,250 dues-paying Mexican members.[51]

Of even greater significance, however, is the case of the International Metalworkers' Federation in Mexico. The IMF is much more active in the country than most other trade secretariats and is the only international trade secretariat which still maintains a regional office in Mexico. Headed by Fernando Melgosa, that office has made notable progress in organizing a National Auto Council "representing almost in its totality, all the automobile plants" in Mexico.[52] As a result, Mexican delegates frequently attend IMF conferences and seminars in the United States. Seminars on auto unionization—one led by Victor Reuther of the United Auto Workers (U.S.A.)—have periodically been sponsored by the IMF in Mexico.[53] Mexican nationals sit on the IMF's executive committees. Moreover, the IMF and its World Auto Councils have allegedly extended financial, as well as cable and letter, support to striking Mexican affiliates—a claim taken up in the "Collective Bargaining" section of this study. But despite its very active presence in the country, the IMF lost its representation at Nissan-Mexicana, the Mexican subsidiary of the Japanese automotive multinational, because of FAT agitation in 1974.[54] The secession of the Nissan-Mexicana union was, in fact, a prime example of FAT rivalry in the labor sector. It reflects the aggressiveness that is becoming commonplace among Mexico's new breed of labor spokesmen.

We shall discuss the Nissan case in more detail later in this study. The important inference here is that Mexican unions may forego international affiliations if local groups aggressively cham-

---

[51] ITF, *XXX Congress, Vienna, 28 July—6 August 1971: Report on Activities for the years 1968, 1969 and 1970* (London: ITF, 1971), pp. 32-33; and ITF, *XXXII Congress*, p. xi. Note: Of the total Mexican membership reported for 1970, all are reported to have paid dues; however, 93,000 allegedly paid affiliation fees at reduced rates.

[52] Raul Castillo, "Trade Union Action—Latin America," *World Company Councils—Auto Workers' Answer to World Company Power* (Geneva: IMF, 1967), p. 20.

[53] IMF, *World Company Councils—Auto Workers' Answer to World Company Power*, p. 43.

[54] Kazutoshi Koshiro, "Comment," in *Multinationals, Unions, and Labor Relations in Industrialized Countries*, ed. Robert F. Banks and Jack Stieber (Ithaca, N.Y.: Cornell University Press, 1977), pp. 140-141. A short version of this article also appeared in the *Japan Labor Bulletin*, February 1, 1975, pp. 5-8.

pion the demands of the rank and file. It is for this reason that Mexican affiliations with international trade secretariats are not at all extensive. In fact, Mexico has more than eight times fewer secretariat members than Brazil, a country where labor affiliations are rigorously monitored by the military government.[55] Given the mounting stress on action-oriented labor representation in Mexico (like that practiced by the FAT), however, it is not surprising that the often weak forms of support which the ITS have to offer—telegrams, solidarity messages, and infrequent trips abroad—simply do not appeal to Mexico's very demanding new generation of unionists.

COLLECTIVE BARGAINING AND THE RIGHT TO STRIKE

Collective bargaining is a major means by which unions in Mexico now assert their power. Mexico's Reformed Labor Law expressly requires employers to bargain collectively with a union if it has membership among their employees and if it "so requests."[56] With over 50 percent of the country's nonagricultural labor force organized at this time, collective bargaining is, therefore, a very common practice. If more than one union claims representation at a plant or firm, the Reformed Labor Law designates the body with the largest representation to act as labor's bargaining agent. Only craftsmen—if they so demand—may be represented by more than one union. Furthermore, the law stipulates the basic format for collective contracts, calling for clauses which establish work times, holiday and rest periods, and salaries. It also affirms the legality of the closed shop, authorizing "exclusion clauses" in collective contracts "by which the employer agrees not to hire any person who is not a member of the union and to discharge any worker who ceases to belong to the union."[57]

Until recently, Mexican unions did not consider the collective bargaining process important. Since minimum wages and working conditions have historically been set by the government in Mexico, unions generally turned to the PRI—not to the bargain-

---

[55] See author's *The Political, Economic, and Labor Climate in Brazil*, Multinational Industrial Relations Series, No. 4A (Philadelphia: Industrial Research Unit, The Wharton School, University of Pennsylvania, 1977), p. 83.

[56] The legal norms for collective bargaining are contained in *Nueva Ley Federal del Trabajo Reformada*, Titulo 7, Capítulo III, Artículos 386-403.

[57] U.S. Department of Labor, *Labor Law and Practice in Mexico*, p. 38.

ing table—for the employment improvements they sought. In recent years, however, the demands of the rank and file have frequently exceeded the concessions which Mexico's inflation-concious governments have been willing to make. As a result, the FAT and other splinter groups have gained rank and file support by injecting considerable militancy into bargaining sessions. Even CTM-affiliated unions are now more demanding during contract negotiations.

Today, collective contracts typically put wages well above the minimums prescribed by the government, prohibit demotions, oblige employers to provide extensive fringe benefits, and establish grievance procedures so that labor disputes can be resolved "in house." For example, the collective contract reached at Volkswagen's Mexican plant for the two-year period 1974-1976 provided for a closed shop, one day's wages per month for punctuality and perfect attendance, a uniform for each employee's use during the May Day solidarity demonstrations, and wages which were as much as 50 percent higher in 1974 than the official minimums in effect in Mexico City in early 1976.[58] When that contract expired in July 1976, FAT partisans organized a VW de Mexico strike to win an additional 20 percent pay boost [59] only months before wages were nationally increased 23 percent by the Echeverría government.[60]

Labor Courts and the Resolution of Labor Disputes

Most disputes involving alleged violations of labor law or contract in Mexico are settled by "labor courts," the country's so-called system of conciliation and arbitration boards. As mentioned previously, grievance procedures are invariably stipulated in collective contracts, so that recourse to the labor courts is usually a last resort endeavor:

> Collective agreements, at least in major industries, commonly contain comprehensive provisions for settling disputes that arise under the contract. Grievances generally must be submitted through the union and various steps and time limits that must be followed may

[58] Sindicato Independiente de Volkswagen de Mexico S.A. de C.V., "Contrato Colectivo de Trabajo," pp. 4, 21, 36, 44-60. (Information on percent wage increase taken from confidential sources.)

[59] See chapter III, n. 51 and n. 52 for further references to this strike.

[60] "Mexico's Wage-Price Policy To Add to Inflationary Woes and Concern Over Peso," *Business Latin America*, September 29, 1976, p. 305.

be prescribed. Joint committees may also be set up to . . . decide on questions of interpretation.[61]

If the in-house machinery set up to resolve disputes does not produce a settlement, either management or labor may seek the help of Mexico's conciliation and arbitration boards. At this stage these labor courts actually function as judicial entities.

Provisions for a network of conciliation and arbitration boards were first made in Mexico's Constitution of 1917. At the present time, Mexico has a dual federal-state system of boards of conciliation (*juntas de conciliación*) and boards of conciliation and arbitration (*juntas de conciliación y arbitraje*). Composed of government, union, and management representatives, these boards function on a permanent basis. They are located throughout Mexico in cities designated by the Labor Ministry (the authority over the federal system) as well as by state governors (the authorities over the respective state or "local" networks). Although they are all vital mediating and enforcement agencies, the federal boards located in Mexico City—the *Junta Central*—are particularly important because of the heavy concentration of industry in the federal district.

Disputes brought to any of these boards are first subject to conciliation efforts. If conciliation is not successful, either party may request arbitration (which is compulsory for employers if workers so demand, but not vice versa). Again, it is only in the arbitration function that Mexico's various *juntas* serve as labor courts per se. If workers reject the arbitration ruling, their contract is terminated, and management can hire replacements in their stead. If management, however, refuses to submit to arbitration or abide by the court's arbitration ruling, the contract is terminated, and the employer must pay each worker twenty days' pay for each year of service plus an additional three months' wages.

Strike plans must be registered with the boards before legal strike action can be taken. In fact, a great many strike plans have been defused because of the labor court's preliminary conciliation efforts. Nevertheless, many local managers have a somewhat dim view of Mexico's labor-court system because of the board's relationship with the dominant political party and, therefore, the unions.

We have already indicated that Mexican labor law is markedly prolabor in tone. It champions the rights of workers in their

---

[61] U.S. Department of Labor, *Labor Law and Practice in Mexico*, p. 39.

relations with employers and embodies the principle of giving preferential treatment to workers whenever interpretation of labor law is in doubt.⟩ Mexico's boards of conciliation and arbitration reflect this same attitude. Mexico's dominant labor confederation, the Mexican Workers' Confederation, is "generally able to elect most of the worker representatives on the boards"; [62] hence most worker representatives on Mexico's labor courts are CTM partisans. This and the CTM's close alliance with Mexico's government have been a vital factor underlying the longevity of PRI rule. Now more than ever, Mexico's government has vested interest in cementing its CTM-labor support. Since "political pressure is applied on the judicial system in Mexico, and little attempt is made to maintain separation of powers," [63] the presence of government and CTM representatives on Mexico's tripartite grievance boards ostensibly gives workers a doubly strong voice. The result, according to some local employers, is that "settlements are obtained through arm twisting that leads in certain cases to excessive concessions in wages and fringe benefits." [64]

In rural areas, local government officials tend to be more closely allied with management; thus, this labor bias is not always apparent in Mexico's outlying state labor courts. In Mexico's industrial areas and federal courts, however, the PRI-CTM alliance is very strong, and board decisions resoundingly favor labor. In fact, Mexican unions are currently campaigning for the abolition of the state board networks to concentrate arbitrations in nationwide, federal labor courts under the jurisdiction of Mexico City. The campaign had added to management's general consensus that workable in-house grievance procedures and conciliation are generally a more pragmatic, often less costly alternative.

The Right to Strike

When internal and labor court efforts fail to resolve worker grievances in Mexico, strike action results. Mexico's Revolution of 1910 erupted in part over the brutal suppression of strikes under the Diaz government, and as a result, the right to strike is

---

[62] *Ibid.*, p. 30.

[63] Alan Riding, "Corruption Again Election Issue in Mexico," *New York Times*, June 29, 1976, p. 2.

[64] Lopez, "Labor and Management," p. 61. Note: Sr. Prieto Lopez's comment refers to the position of "some employers" in Mexico—not to his own.

rigorously defended by the Constitution of 1917 and by all subsequent labor legislation.

The Constitution of 1917 broadly defines a lawful strike to include virtually any walkout "whose aim is to balance the different factors of production, harmonizing the rights of labor with the rights of capital." [65] Strikes are constitutionally unlawful "only when the majority of the striking workers practice acts of violence" or when civil servants declare a strike against a government organ in a time of war. Employer shutdowns or "lockouts," however, are expressly forbidden by the constitution unless a conciliation and arbitration board tacitly approves of such work stoppage as a means of curbing excess production and stabilizing market prices.[66]

Subsequent labor laws have extended these basic provisions and defined strike and lockout legality in much greater detail. In the case of strikes, a series of notification procedures and conciliation attempts are now prerequisite for lawful strike action. These are reviewed in the following section to illustrate the dynamics and scope of strike action under current Mexican law.

Strike Logistics in Mexico

Current labor law stipulates that a series of "pre-strike" conditions must be met before lawful strike action can be initiated.[67] First, a written strike notice citing labor's grievances must be submitted to management and to the appropriate board of conciliation and arbitration having jurisdiction in the area. Employers must receive this notice at least six days prior to the walkout (ten days in the case of public services). In the interim, the labor court must attempt to resolve the dispute by conciliation. If no settlement is reached, either management or labor may request a court arbitration ruling, although labor has the right to veto an arbitration proceeding if it is sought by management. At the same time, a majority of workers must approve the strike call. This majority is determined on the total number of employees, including all former workers discharged after the

---

[65] *Constitución Política de los Estados Unidos Mexicanos,* TITULO 6, ARTICULOS 18, 19.

[66] *Ibid.*

[67] The procedures cited above for strike application in Mexico were synthesized from U.S. Department of Labor, *Labor Law and Practice in Mexico,* pp. 39-41. Readers desiring further particulars on Mexican strike logistics are urged to consult that text.

written strike application is served, but excluding any new workers who may be hired afterward. Finally, labor's strike intent must be predicated on one of four motives if the strike is to be legal: (1) to obtain "equilibrium" as expressed in the Constitutition of 1917—now interpreted to mean achievement of the same working conditions as those offered by similar concerns operating in the local; (2) to force management to negotiate a collective contract or to honor an existing one; (3) to extract a revision of a collective contract upon its expiration; or (4) to demonstrate labor solidarity as in the case of sympathy strikes.

If these requirements are met, but labor's grievances are not resolved at the labor court, a strike may legally ensue. Even then, management, workers, or third parties have the right to petition the labor court to nullify the strike on the grounds that its preliminary requirements were not met or that the strike violates a clause of a valid collective agreement. Should the labor court concur, the strike is declared "non-existent," and workers are given twenty-four hours to return to their jobs before their contract terminates. If the strike is decreed lawful (*i.e.*, "existent" in Mexican legal parlance), however, all employment contracts are suspended, and no replacements can be hired. Legal strike action can continue indefinitely; it can only be stopped by mutual agreement, by a labor court's arbitration ruling, or by the mutually acceptable ruling of a third party.

Although local officials are quick to point out that strikes are often averted under Mexico's conciliation and arbitration system, Mexican strike militancy has stepped up in recent years. Between 1950 and 1960, for example, Mexico had an annual average of 235 strikes, typically involving about 31,000 workers.[68] By 1974, however, the threat of national strikes triggered by the CTM and involving millions of workers had become a frequent concern:

> During the latter part of both 1973 and in 1974, unions used the threat of national strikes to have their emergency wage increase demands met. Only a few strikes actually materialized because companies granted most of the demands with the strong encourage-

---

[68] The average numbers of strikes and workers involved per year were computed from data from Secretaría del Trabajo y Prevision Social, *Memoria de Labores* (Mexico, D.F.: STPS 1956 and 1962) ; and Secretaría de Industria y Comercio, *Anuario Estadístico de los Estados Unidos Mexicanos, 1960-1961* (Mexico, D.F.: Dirección General de Estadística, 1963), Table 8.4, p. 332.

ment of the Echeverria administration. The issue of the legality of these strikes never arose because the Echeverria administration was apparently unwilling to arouse union hostility.[69]

Since the early 1970s, moreover, many multinational firms in Mexico—General Motors, Nissan, Volkswagen, General Electric, and Spicer, to name a few—have been hit by a rash of prolonged strikes. These disputes have often been organized by militant splinter groups to rival CTM-affiliated unions for power or by outside agitators for their own profit.

Professional strike organization has become common in Mexico and is a lucrative business. Since most strike settlements give workers a percentage of the pay which they lost during a walkout, there are many professional agitators who organize strikes in exchange for a percentage of this "backpay." As a result, United States businessmen with experience in the country report that "some strikes get going where the gates are simply blocked even though the workers want to go back to work." [70] This practice became particularly prevalent under the Echeverría government when legal strike requirements were often ignored. Violence is also commonplace, so that other multinational professionals relate incidents of gun-brandishing strike organizers "encouraging" workers to go along with their strike demands. Because of the fear of violence and particularly because of the Mexican public's deep "revolutionary" respect for labor, picket lines in Mexico are rigorously honored.

Strike action is also a tactic increasingly used by splinter labor groups in the country to rally the rank and file away from traditional, CTM-affiliated unions. A review of the strikes recently staged at General Motors' and Nissan's plants in Mexico illustrates how splinter groups assert their power and how strike action is now used in the country for onerous labor gains.

The 1974 and 1976 Nissan-Mexicana Strikes

Nissan-Mexicana, located in Cuernavaca, is a subsidiary of the second largest Japanese automobile firm. It suffered strikes in 1974 and 1976 which illustrate both the increasing labor militancy in Mexico and the relations of Mexican labor with international labor groups.

---

[69] Business International Corp., "Mexico," *Investing, Licensing, and Trading Conditions Abroad*, October 1975, p. 21.

[70] Author's conversation with United States industrial relations specialist with recent experience in Mexico.

The 1974 strike began on April 1 and ended twenty-one days later. The principal issue was wages. The union demanded an 80 percent increase, the company offered 17 percent, and the settlement provided for a 22 percent increase. The labor agreement was for two years; and when it expired on April 1, 1976, the union again struck, this time for forty-seven days. Again the basic issue was wages—the union demanding a 40 percent increase, the company offering 15 percent; this time a settlement of 20 percent was reached.[71]

The moving force behind these strikes has been the Authentic Workers Federation (FAT) which won control of the Nissan-Mexicana local union prior to the 1974 strike and which also controls the locals at Volkswagen and at DINA Nacional. The FAT is a Marxist Christian-Democratic, radical group which is affiliated with the *Confederación Latinamericana Sindical Cristiana* (CLAS), headquartered in Venezuela, and with the World Confederation of Labour, headquartered in Brussels. The FAT opposes Mexico's labor hierarchy and relationships with the secretariats, including the IMF, and is aggressively antagonistic toward multinational firms. Nevertheless, it has maintained at least a nominal membership in the IMF Nissan World Council.

The 1974 Strike. There are several accounts of the 1974 strike. According to Professor Koshiro:

> The union of Nissan Mexicana used to be affiliated to the IMF, but the left-wing faction within the union manipulated its secession from both IMF and the Mexican TUC, demanding a tremendous wage increase of 80 percent. Since the union still remained a member of the NWAC [Nissan World Auto Council], however, Ichiro Shioji, president of the JAW [Japan Auto Workers] and the NWAC, took advantage of this situation to mediate in the dispute. As a result, a 22 percent increase was accepted.[72]

---

[71] This strike has been commented upon by the *IMF News*, No. 16 (May 1974), p. 1 and No. 22 (June 1974), p. 7; by Professor Koshiro, Yokohama National University, "Comment," in *Multinationals, Unions, and Labor Relations*, pp. 138-145; and by Burton Bendiner, Coordinator of the IMF Automotive World Councils, "World Automotive Councils: A Union Response to Transnational Bargaining," in *Multinationals, Unions, and Labor Relations*, pp. 186-191. Because of some factual discrepancies, the Industrial Research Unit discussed the facts and issues with officials of Nissan and the Japanese Confederation of Automobile Unions in Tokyo, July 1977, and with officials of Nissan-Mexicana, Mexico City, August 1977.

[72] Koshiro, "Comment," pp. 140-141. Koshiro stated that Mexican Ford and Volkswagen had already reached an agreement for a 20 percent increase. Actually, Ford did not have a negotiation in 1974, and Volkswagen settled three months after Nissan for 24 percent.

The IMF also claimed considerable involvement in the 1974 strike:

> Coordinated efforts through the IMF Nissan World Auto Council in Geneva, by Ichiro Shioji, President of Jidosha Soren, the Confederation of Japan Automobile Unions, Ivar Norén, IMF General Secretary and Fernando Melgosa, IMF Regional Representative for Latin America, resulted in a settlement including a 22 per cent increase for Nissan workers in the Cuernavaca plant in Mexico. An unreasonable stance by the Company, in first making a contemptuous offer of only 1 per cent increase [*sic*] in the face of the union's demand for a 20-30 per cent wage rise [*sic*], was overcome by the efforts of all concerned, spearheaded by the union leaders in the plant itself.[73]

A later IMF publication corrected the account to note that the company offered 15 percent, not 1 percent.[74] The coordinator of the IMF World Automotive Councils summarized the series of events involving the 1974 strike as follows:

> The Coordinator's office in Geneva was informed by cable by the IMF representative in Mexico City that the union at the Cuernavacos [*sic*] plant was on strike, involving about 1,300 workers. A wage increase was the chief issue; the union and management were far apart and an impasse had developed. In addition, there were complicating factors in the local situation: a group of dissidents was determined to embarrass the local union leadership.
> A first step was to inform Ichiro Shioji, president of the Confederation of Japanese Auto Workers and head of the Nissan Auto Workers' Union in Japan. Shioji helped the IMF inform the Nissan and Toyota Councils. When the issues were made clear to him, Shioji discussed the Mexican union's demands with the parent company's industrial relations department and with top management dealing with the company's Mexican subsidiary. Shioji had the backing of his own union and of the confederation, but he also had to listen to the Tokyo office's side of the story and to the version that it had received from the local management in Mexico City. This information was sent to the Geneva office and relayed to Cuernavacos [*sic*]. After denials, further explanations, clarifications, and eventual concessions on both sides, a final settlement was made 7 per cent above the local management's original offer.
> Although it was not global union agreement, it was coordinated collective bargaining—Mexico City, Geneva, and Tokyo. A settlement would have been possible without the IMF Nissan World Auto Council, but undeniably it would have been a lot more difficult for the weaker Mexican affiliate of the IMF to reach satisfactory terms

---

[73] "Nissan Mexicana Conflict Settled," *IMF News*, No. 16 (May 1974), p. 1.

[74] *Ibid.*, No. 22 (June 1974), p. 7.

with the company. Also, it would have taken a good deal longer, were it not for the assistance of the stronger Japanese union.[75]

The Industrial Research Unit's investigation indicates that the IMF role, as Mr. Bendiner reported, was limited, but that of the Japanese Confederation of Automobile Unions, more extensive. The FAT group has been more ready to permit the Japanese Confederation a role than to deal through the IMF. Moreover, the Japanese Confederation officials did not take a strong position in the situation, but primarily attempted to ascertain the facts and to inform Nissan headquarters of what they learned and of their position regarding the dispute. They were an information channel, but certainly not a part of a coordinated bargaining effort. There was no action, nor threats of action, against Nissan plants in Japan, or those in any other part of the world. The dispute settlement, although very high, was in line with previous bargains by Ford, Volkswagen, and other companies in the Mexican automobile industry.

The 1976 Strike. There appears to have been no IMF involvement in the 1976 strike. No mention of this strike appears in the 1976 issues of the *IMF News Bulletin.* No Mexican union delegation attended the Nissan World Council meeting in Japan in 1975.[76] This could be because of lack of funds, as well as ideological differences, but the FAT group was still in control of the Nissan-Mexicana local in 1976 and led the strike which produced approximately the same results as the 1974 strike. The Japanese Confederation of Automobile Unions maintained some contact with the local union during the strike, as they still do, which again, has been informational in character and limited by ideological differences.

As these strikes illustrate, Mexican labor is beset with divisions; and in some areas, radical groups are in the ascent. This both complicates international union relationships and requires that claims of international union action be carefully scrutinized.

The 1973, 1975, and 1977 General Motors Strikes

The recent experience of General Motors in Mexico has been somewhat different, but is also noteworthy. General Motors has

---

[75] Bendiner, "World Automotive Councils," pp. 187-188.

[76] IMF, "Revised: Participants," Nissan and Toyota World Auto Councils, Second Meeting, Gotemba City, Japan, October 13-15, 1975. (Mimeographed.)

two plants operating in Mexico—one in Mexico City and another in Toluca, thirty-five miles away from the capital. The unions representing GM's workers at these plants are CROC and CTM affiliates, respectively. Some Mexican sources suggest that GM is currently a target for FAT infiltration. While that claim is extremely difficult to substantiate, the escalation of strike militancy at GM's Mexican facilities is not. The fact is that GM suffered no strikes in Mexico between 1965 and 1973. Since 1973, however, strike action has taken a very heavy toll on GM's Mexican operations.

GM entered 1973 with an "indefinite contract" with its Mexican employees. Its 1971 collective contract became two years old in February 1973 and would have been extended automatically for another two years had neither management nor labor demanded its revision. Labor at GM's Mexico City plant, however, made clear its demand for higher wages in January 1973. By February 13, a strike was in effect. It lasted five days, but resulted in significant gains for GM's workers. Wages were increased 15 percent, and 50 percent strike pay was authorized. Company-paid life insurance coverage was increased 14 percent. Company contributions to a workers' savings program were increased 40 percent.[77]

These gains, however, did not wholly appease GM's rank and file unionists. Two years later, on February 17, 1975, they staged yet another strike, much to management's dismay. That strike lasted twenty-eight days and reportedly received the financial backing of the Mexican Labor Congress, the International Metalworkers' Federation (IMF), and the United Auto Workers (UAW).[78] Specifically, the IMF's Geneva office allegedly contributed US$2,000 to GM's striking workers, and UAW President Leonard Woodcock, "who is also President of the IMF Automotive Department, cabled $5,000."[79] The walkout was only ended, moreover, when GM's management agreed to a 13 per-

---

[77] Alberto Gomez Obregon, Personnel Director of Labor, interview held at General Motors plant in Mexico City, August 24, 1977. The IMF claimed that 55 percent strike pay was authorized, and that a company-subsidized meal service was implemented. "New Agreement GM Mexico," *IMF News*, No. 9 (February 1973), p. 2. (The meal service, however, was already in effect.)

[78] "Mexico—Latest Development on GM Strike," *IMF News*, No. 5 (March 1975), p. 1.

[79] "The IMF and the General Motors Strike in Mexico," Circular Letter No. 14 of Herman Rebhan, IMF General Secretary, March 18, 1975.

cent wage increase (retroactive to February with 55 percent
strike pay), an increase in the yearly bonus paid workers for
punctuality and regular attendance from an equivalent 37 to 39
days' wages.[80]

So successful was this strike action that GM's 2,500 employees
at the Mexico City plant ventured it a third time in 1977 for
further benefit and wage gains. Demanding a 24 percent pay
increase, company payment of employee income taxes, and higher
social security benefits, GM's workers struck on February 8,
1977, at a time when the government-labor covenant for a 10
percent wage-increase ceiling was theoretically in effect.[81] Management offered to increase wages by 5.8 percent and to boost
workers' life insurance and sick pay coverage. After some one
million man-hours were lost, however, GM's managers were forced
to up the ante. As reported earlier in this study, workers
finally settled for a wage increase of 10 percent (retroactive
to February 8 at 50 percent).[82] Although the settlement represented no great victory for the workers, United States publications reported that:

> Mexican auto makers are breathing a sigh of relief at last week's
> settlement of a bitter 62-day strike at General Motors of Mexico.
> The GM settlement, which sets the pattern for the other car compa-
> nies, calls for a 10% wage hike. . . . But even that 10% may prove
> too high for some members of the embattled industry.[83]

Since 1973, then, General Motors has been hit by three strikes
in Mexico. Not coincidentally, GM has shown no profits in
Mexico since 1973. In fact, the company lost US$5 million on
sales of US$260 million in 1976, owing to its high labor and
component costs on top of the government's contraction of credit
for auto buyers.[84]

The General Motors and Nissan strikes illustrate the upsurge
in labor militancy that is taking place in Mexico. Mexican unions,
which typically relied on government decrees to gain higher

---

[80] "Mexico—Settlement at GM," *IMF News*, No. 6 (March 1975), p. 2.

[81] "GM Says Strike at Plant in Mexico City Is Ended," *Wall Street Journal*,
April 13, 1977, p. 11.

[82] Alberto Gomez Obregon, Personnel Director of Labor, interview held at
General Motors plant in Mexico City, August 24, 1977.

[83] "Mexico—Why the Auto Makers Are Taking a Beating," *Business Week*,
May 2, 1977, p. 41.

[84] *Ibid.*, pp. 41, 44.

wages, are turning more and more to strike threats and strike action to gain their wage demands. As the Nissan case makes additionally clear, this strike activity may be spearheaded by militant splinter groups which even the international trade secretariats have found troublesome. It is this kind of labor militancy which signals the loss of control of Mexico's traditional labor leaders over the rank and file. It not only jeopardizes the industrial climate in Mexico, but threatens the country's vital labor-government alliance as well.

FEDERAL GOVERNMENT AND ORGANIZED LABOR TIES

There is frequently debate in publications on Mexico over whether the government controls labor or whether labor controls the government. Indeed, the relationship between the two is so complex that it is genuinely difficult to assert the "dominance" of one body over the other. Two facts are, however, clear. First, government and labor vitally depend on each other in Mexico. Without the close support of the other, neither group could maintain its power or prestige. Second, this labor-government interdependence is the product of long historical evolution and of Mexico's Revolutionary mythology. As one publication states, "In domestic policy, [Fidel] Velázquez would describe the relationship of the CTM to the government as reciprocal, each helping the other and thereby strengthening the Revolution." [85]

Indeed, following the Revolution of 1910, it became an established tradition in Mexico that "the Mexican labor movement would actively participate in the country's political life." [86] Mexico's government party has long attempted to include all organized labor groups in its supportive labor sector. The Mexican Labor Congress and the Labor Unity Bloc (BUO) are largely the products of this centralization or unification drive. While the labor groups incorporated in these bodies have often feuded for organizational dominance, all of them have cultivated strong ties with the PRI.

---

[85] Harvey A. Levenstein, *Labor Organizations in the United States and Mexico* (Westport, Conn.: Greenwood Publishing Co., 1971), p. 223, citing CTM, *Informe al LVIII Consejo Nacional*, 1958, p. 4.

[86] Alexander, *Organized Labor in Latin America*, p. 193.

Today, the intertwining of labor and government in Mexico is very complex. The CTM is an autonomous labor entity, but it is also the PRI's semiofficial labor arm and the spokesman for the Party's large labor sector. Like the Labor Congress and the Labor Unity Bloc, the CTM gives Mexico's government vital election support. Mexico's "most important labor leaders are in a very real sense members of the small group which in fact governs Mexico." [87] Mexico's government, however, exerts considerable formal control over organized labor by its enactment and enforcement of labor legislation. Informally, of course, government patronage is also a significant control mechanism. The federal government has absolute jurisdiction over labor disputes involving more than one state or occurring in the federal district. Federal wage adjustments have traditionally been aimed at currying labor support and promoting union growth. Candidates for most key union posts require congressional nomination (although many Mexican congressmen are, themselves, CTM appointees). Conversely, all top civil service positions require union membership.

In these respects, organized labor and PRI government maintain a symbiotic relationship that is one of the most important but least understood characteristics of Mexican society. Even more significant, however, is the fact that changes in this relationship are now in the making. Rank and file dissent is already apparent in the labor sector. Workers, accustomed to the generous wage adjustments of the Echeverría administration, are disgruntled with the effects of inflation on their incomes and with the limitation on wage gains which had been in effect. Together with Mexico's peasants, they were incensed by López Portillo's recent expulsion of peasants from expropriated land. Mexico's agricultural problems—low productivity and inefficient, subsistence farming under the *ejido* system—have particularly brought peasants and some workers into hostile confrontations with the PRI machine. Too, Mexican laborers have been alienated by the widespread corruption that is apparent in government and trade union circles.

These various undercurrents have had two important repercussions in Mexico. There appears to be a movement toward active, young, militant labor leaders, and Mexican workers seem to be looking for a new breed of labor spokesmen to voice

[87] *Ibid.*, p. 197.

their demands and to curb the abuses of power apparently practiced. At the same time, traditional labor groups—and, with them, the PRI—are losing rank and file support. As one publication phrased it:

> Labor is restless: urban industrial workers are less and less willing to rely on the traditional chain of labor command to protect their interests. Labor's expectations have been inflated by four years of government support under former President Luis Echeverria Alvarez, but at the same time its realizations have suffered from inflation and unemployment.[88]

These repercussions are accentuated by the age of and apparent lack of an heir for Fidel Velázquez. As has been pointed out, a leadership vacuum in the CTM could result, further exacerbating the changes that might occur in government-labor relationships.

---

[88] "Mexico: The Next Five Years," *Business International*, March 18, 1977, p. 84.

CHAPTER V

Conclusions—1977

Mexico is unique among most Latin American countries in that it boasts a broad industrial infrastructure and a forty-seven year-old record of single party government. For many years, in fact, Mexico attracted extensive multinational investments because of its economic growth, political stability, and stable exchange rate with the United States dollar. Recently, however, symptoms of Mexican economic malaise have become apparent in Mexico proper as well as in its neighbor to the north:

> Increased unemployment here, for example, has forced more Mexicans to enter the United States illegally to look for work. The economic slump has meant lower imports from the United States. The peso devaluation has badly hit [United States] border states because fewer Mexican tourists can now afford dollar prices. Mexico's shaky credit standing has worried United States bankers with huge portfolios here.[1]

As a result, multinational businessmen are today "much more sober and guarded" in their assessment of Mexico's investment potential and economic future.[2]

To evaluate Mexico's business climate accurately, however, a careful look at the country's labor sector is a critical prerequisite. Organized labor and PRI government are the two key power blocs in modern day Mexico. Each vitally depends on the other, yet both have been driven toward different corners in recent years largely because of inflation and government efforts to check it. Mexico's current administration is therefore attempting to persuade labor to accept austerity measures in the economy. President López Portillo has stressed the need for a cold, realistic approach toward wage adjustments and the curbing of inflation.

---

[1] Alan Riding, ". . . Mexico Also Has Its Difficulties," *New York Times*, February 20, 1977, p. A-5.

[2] Thomas E. Mullaney, "Optimism and Hope on Outlook in Mexico," *New York Times*, December 17, 1976, p. D-11.

148

"The private sector," according to one report, "is being urged to create new jobs . . ., trade unionists are being told that wages must be held down." [3] In the case of the unions, however, this approach has strained Mexico's crucial labor-government alliance.

The vital problem put forth by this study is that Mexico's traditional labor leadership—and, as a result, Mexico's PRI government as well—appears to be losing control over the country's all-important labor sector. Labor militancy is escalating in the country, and splinter groups, such as the FAT, are attracting more and more of the rank and file. A new generation of Mexican workers, placated by the high wage adjustments of the Echeverría regime and used to getting its way, is clearly "in no mood to start making sacrifices now." [4] Mexico's traditional labor leaders are increasingly following—not leading—the wage and benefit campaigns of these workers.

Compounding this situation is the prospect of CTM leadership problems in the near future. The CTM, the huge confederation which has mustered most of the PRI's labor support, is faced with an inevitable leadership contest which is likely to cause serious conflicts between CTM-PRI partisans.

Given these factors—the power erosion of Mexico's traditional labor leadership, the suspect future of CTM leadership, the various economic problems which Mexico is now confronting, and the plan of attack thus far implemented by Mexico's government to improve the economic climate—Mexico's investment and labor outlooks are both questionable. Put simply, Mexico can go one of two routes: the government can opt for a stronger economy at the continued expense of its labor support; conversely, the PRI regime can opt for labor appeasement and improved labor support at the expense of faster economic recovery. It is the consensus of several analyses and this study that the latter option is perhaps the more likely:

> . . . the government is confronted with difficult choices. It might be able to win or to force allegiance from dissident labor groups, but only at the risk of shortening fuses. The government now

---

[3] Alan Riding, "Lopez Portillo's Struggle," *Financial Times*, December 18, 1976, p. 5.

[4] Alan Riding, "Mexico's Inflation Fight: Stomach vs. Program," *New York Times*, April 16, 1977, p. 33.

appears more likely to sacrifice some of its economic goals to mollify labor dissent.[5]

Revenues from Mexico's extensive petroleum reserves, however, may help the country surmount most economic setbacks in the next few years. How the government handles its new resources could enable it to resolve the labor-economy dilemma.

---

[5] "Mexico: The Next Five Years," *Business International*, March 18, 1977, p. 84. This view is also expressed in Mullaney, "Optimism and Hope," p. D-11.

CHAPTER VI

Conclusions—1977 to 1980

Significant developments from 1977 to 1979 in Mexico's economic and industrial policies, its domestic politics, the labor scene, and Mexican-United States relations confirm much of the preceding chapters' assessment. The oil and natural gas discoveries of the last two years have created new options for the country in dealing with domestic issues and in relations with the rest of the world. Jorge Díaz Serrano, executive director of the government-owned petroleum monopoly, PEMEX (Petróleos Mexicanos), has aptly described Mexico's current position, "Notwithstanding the risk, it is better to face problems generated by wealth than those caused by poverty." [1] Nevertheless, that very wealth may serve to highlight problems such as unemployment, illegal immigration, inflation, and the widening socioeconomic gap between the rich and the poor. Therefore, Mexico's political structure is challenged not only by economic demands but by social pressures as well.

POLITICAL DEVELOPMENTS

President López Portillo's competent administration has earned Mexico a good reputation in the international community through sound debt management, substantial economic growth, and the creation of a favorable investment climate. Hydrocarbon resources are the basis for strengthening commercial ties with Europe and Japan; however, the administration intends to strengthen and diversify Mexico's trade in other raw materials and manufactured goods. In addition, as a result of oil wealth and a stable political system, Mexico is in a very good position to assume Third World leadership. [2]

---

[1] Anthony J. Parisi, "Economic and Political Concerns Could Slow Tide of Mexican Oil," *New York Times*, February 13, 1979, p. D-15.

[2] "Business Outlook, Mexico," *Business Latin America*, July 18, 1979, p. 228.

On the domestic political front, unions are still restless, and if less-than-inflation wage restraints continue, "serious labor strife could develop." [3] The political ramifications of labor dissatisfaction are not insignificant, for the close relationship between the ruling political party, the *Partido Revolucionario Institucional* (PRI), and the most powerful union organization in Mexico, the *Confederación de Trabajadores de México* (CTM), still exists. Political shifts to the left within the ranks of the CTM could extend to the broader political scene.

In 1978, in a move designed to ease social pressures and democratize the political process, López Portillo legalized opposition parties, among them the *Partido Comunista de México* (PCM) and the *Partido Demócrata Mexicano* (PDM). Also, in an electoral reform measure instituted prior to the July 1, 1979, congressional election, the number of seats awarded on a proportional representation basis was raised from 40 to 100.[4] The PRI won 296 out of 300 constituency seats; the right-wing Catholic *Partido de Acción Nacional* (PAN) won 4 constituency seats and 40 on the basis of proportional representation; the PCM received 18 seats; the *Partido Popular Socialista* (PPS) won 12 seats; the *Partido Auténtico de la Revolución Mexicana* (PARM) won 11 seats; and the *Partido Socialista de los Trabajadores* (PST) and the extreme right-wing PDM won 9 seats apiece.[5]

Although providing some diversity in political choice, this election elicited one of the poorest voter turnouts in recent years. The high abstention rate (various sources estimate anywhere from 40 percent to more than 50 percent of the 28 million electorate did not participate) is a sign of general disillusion. Reportedly, with an eye toward a reorganization of the party, the PRI national committee has undertaken a study of the party's electoral performance.

The CTM leadership, i.e., Fidel Velázquez, sees no need for change in the basic PRI policies but rather a need for more effective implementation of those policies.[6] Nevertheless, there are some undercurrents of leftist sentiment within labor's ranks,

---

[3] *Ibid.*, p. 230.

[4] William Chislett, "Aftermath of Mexico's General Election, Few Happy with Results," *Financial Times*, July 19, 1979, p. 3.

[5] *Ibid.*

[6] "Mexico: Inglorious Victory," *Latin America Political Report*, August 10, 1979, p. 246.

which is mirrored in the PRI itself and may not be satisfied with intraparty reform or more effective implementation. In fact, leftist factions within the PRI have recently allied themselves with left-wing parties on certain issues.[7] These undercurrents will take on more significance if the leadership of the CTM is challenged when Velázquez stands for reelection in 1980. For the near term, however, the PRI will maintain its dominance, and the current administration can be expected to chart a moderate political course.

MEXICAN-UNITED STATES RELATIONS

Contemporary relations between the United States and Mexico are determined by three important issues: energy, immigration, and trade.

Energy

In light of the rising estimates of petroleum and natural gas reserves, currently placed at some 45 billion barrels of known petroleum and associated natural gas reserves and 200 billion barrels of potential reserves,[8] Mexico has grown in importance as a supplier not only to the United States but to the world as well. The course of oil development as being charted by President López Portillo involves a controlled production with revenues channeled into targeted sectors of the economy. The ranking of priorities, the level and pace of funding, and the need to control domestic inflationary pressures while stimulating employment are some of the obstacles that López Portillo must overcome to capitalize on Mexico's resource wealth on an international basis and to preserve domestic peace and prosperity. Exports of oil and natural gas will contribute significantly to the growth of Gross Domestic Product (see Tables A-1 and A-3), but the distribution of the resulting wealth will be of major interest. Mexico does not intend to follow the example of Saudi Arabia and Iran in acquiring sophisticated armaments.[9] Rather, it will

---

[7] Business International Corporation, "Mexico," *Investing, Licensing, and Trading Conditions Abroad*, April 1978, p. 2.

[8] "López Portillo Stresses Aggressive Growth for Mexican Economy," *Business Latin America*, September 5, 1979, p. 281.

[9] Alan Riding, "Mexico's Oil Won't Solve All the Problems," *New York Times*, February 4, 1979, p. 72.

commit oil income to the development of the infrastructure, the import of capital goods, and the reduction of the more than $30 billion foreign debt. President López Portillo has stated: "This opportunity to get oil will come only once in history. We have to transform a non-renewable resource into a permanent source of wealth." [10]

The established Mexican policy of gearing oil exports to Mexico's needs and its policy on natural gas exports, which was announced just prior to the September 1979 meeting between Presidents López Portillo and Carter, illustrate Mexico's more confident attitude in its dealings with the United States. In 1977, the United States flatly rejected the proposed sale of natural gas, largely because of a stalemate on the contract price. This proved to be a short-sighted decision for a number of reasons. First, because natural gas reserves are associated with oil reserves, increasing oil production (which would be advantageous from the United States' perspective) would yield an even greater surplus of natural gas than now exists. Second, the Mexican supplies have the advantage of geographical proximity and security. Third, the joint efforts to develop the natural gas transportation and delivery system could have resulted in employment and income for both the United States and Mexico. Mexico, however, has put the pipeline in place (with some support from Japan) and is using the natural gas to fuel its electric power plants, with only the surplus being allocated for export. Consequently, the 1979 agreement allows for a smaller volume of natural gas export (300 million cubic feet per day) than was originally planned and at a price of over $3.60 per 1,000 cubic feet,[11] which will be tied to the increase in the world oil price.

Immigration

Immigration is a controversial issue on both sides of the border. Because of critical pressures placed on the Mexican job market by a population growing at a rate of 3.2 percent a year, illegal emigration, viewed from the Mexican perspective, is a necessary safety valve. In the United States, conflicting interests exist. The labor provided by illegal aliens is in many cases a

---

[10] William Chislett, "Oil Production on a Giant Scale," *Financial Times*, November 2, 1978, p. 26.

[11] "Six U.S. Firms to Buy Mexican Natural Gas," *Wall Street Journal*, October 22, 1979, p. 14.

boon to employers, but it is also perceived as a threat to the strength of American labor unions. The various government agencies cannot agree on a coherent policy because of conflicting special interests. For example, the Agriculture Department wants to control food imports from Mexico but not the flow of poorly paid, illegal farmworkers. The Labor Department, on the other hand, lobbies for an inexpensive food supply but wants to curb illegal immigration.[12] Some United States economists note, however, that immigrant labor has become essential to this country because not only do these workers fill employment needs in unskilled and generally low-paying jobs that United States citizens may not want but they also contribute to the economy through sales taxes, social security contributions, and income taxes.[13]

Certain developments in the United States have influenced the flow of immigrants, such as enactment of the minimum wage law and the increase in welfare payments relative to market wages.[14] These developments have permitted illegal aliens to move into jobs at the bottom of the wage structure. If immigrant labor were abolished, the low-wage work force would be reduced; wages would be driven up; and the number of jobs would be reduced, particularly in the service and agricultural sectors. Mexico's economy would lose as well because the repatriated labor force would depress wage scales even further, aggravate unemployment, and the income from work in the United States would be lost.

Although it is logical for the United States and Mexico to combine efforts to deal with the situation of illegal immigration, there is still a great deal of resistance in the United States to allowing Mexicans easier access to the job market. The concerns that Mexican workers take jobs from United States citizens, challenge union strength, and lower the wage standard are real and very emotional issues. In his conversations with President Carter early in 1979, Mexico's López Portillo suggested a possible answer to the problem in reinstituting the *bracero*, or guest immigrant worker program, which was discontinued in 1964.

---

12 "Mexico and the United States: Why come then?" *Economist*, February 10, 1979, p. 79.

13 William Stevens, "Millions of Mexicans View Illegal Entry to U.S. as Door to Opportunity," *New York Times*, February 12, 1979, p. 1.

14 Michael L. Wachter, "Second Thoughts About Illegal Immigration," *Fortune*, May 22, 1978, pp. 80-87.

The issue was raised again in the September 1979 talks; however, no decision emerged.

Trade

Mexico and the United States are inextricably linked in trade. In fact, according to one White House aide, "Mexico has a greater impact on the United States than does any other country." [15] Mexico is the United States' best market in Latin America and the fifth largest trading partner in the world, and in 1978, the United States received over 60 percent of Mexico's total exports.[16]

Aided by United States tax provisions that allow component parts from the United States to be imported and the product to be assembled in Mexico and by Mexican investment laws, Mexico's border industries program is flourishing. Only the "value added" in Mexico is subject to United States import duties. At present, there are some 470 in-bond plants, or *maquiladoras*, operating along Mexico's northern border, and 60 new in-bond plants are currently operating throughout the country.[17] From the United States' perspective, these plants offer indigenous employment, helping to reduce the influx of illegal immigrants, and offer the production of goods at favorable wage and tax rates. For Mexico, the in-bond industries strengthen the infrastructure, provide much-needed employment and job training at home, and contribute to the national income. The in-bond industries reflect the emerging assertive attitude in Mexico toward trading relations with the United States, an attitude verbalized by President López Portillo: "What Mexico needs is time to find jobs for its people. Mexico does not want to export workers. It wants to export goods." [18]

---

[15] Martin Tolchin, "Washington Seeking to Repair Schism with New Powerful, Oil Rich Mexico," *New York Times*, February 9, 1979, p. A-52.

[16] U.S., Department of Commerce, Bureau of the Census, *Highlights of U.S. Export and Import Trade*, Vol. FT 990 (Washington, D.C.: U.S. Government Printing Office, 1979), Tab. I-6, p. 88.

[17] Martha Lowenstern, *Profile of Labor Conditions: Mexico* (Washington, D.C.: U.S., Department of Labor, Bureau of International Affairs, 1979), p. 3.

[18] James Reston, "Mexico Wants Full Review of Ties in Carter Talks," *New York Times*, February 8, 1979, p. A-12.

ECONOMIC AND INDUSTRIAL DEVELOPMENT

An assessment of Mexico's economic health at this midpoint in President López Portillo's administration would yield generally optimistic results. Using Gross Domestic Product (GDP) as a benchmark, Mexico's stagnant economy of 1976 gave way to a 3.2 percent increase in real terms for 1977 and grew by 6.6 percent in 1978.[19] According to forecasts prepared by DIEMEX-Wharton Econometric Forecasting Associates, growth for 1979 will be on the average of 7.3 percent, with a more moderate rate in 1980 of 6.6 percent (see Table A-1).

In the last quarter of 1979, the fast-growing Mexican stock exchange, *Bolsa de Valores,* was in the midst of a boom, having recovered from some skittish selling in May and June of 1979 (see Figure VI-1). The main cause for the drop in the index was that, in the first five months of 1979, new stock issues amounted to P8.4 billion, compared to P7 billion for all of 1978.[20] Clearly, the *Bolsa* is still a "thin" exchange; that is, speculation causes repercussions that might not be as noticeable in an exchange trading a larger index of stocks. Nevertheless, with inflation projected to continue at a high rate, the issue of stock should prove a less inflationary alternative than bank loans for firms seeking to raise capital while providing investors with good returns on the market. Accordingly, the trend is increasing for companies to issue stock rather than follow traditional debt financing.

Another positive sign of Mexico's economic strength and policy direction is that external borrowing, with some pressure from the International Monetary Fund, was kept within the $3 billion guideline for 1978 and was declining to something over $2 billion for 1979.[21] In addition, Mexico has restructured large portions of foreign debt by replacing existing five-year loans with loans maturing in ten years or more and bearing lower interest rates for an annual saving of about $33 million in interest charges.[22] Foreign investment in Mexico is estimated at $5 to $6 billion and is concentrated in the most dynamic areas of the economy,

---

[19] Donald D. Holt, "Why the Bankers Suddenly Love Mexico," *Fortune,* July 16, 1979, p. 140.

[20] "Mexican Bolsa is a Timely Reminder of Market Volatility," *Business Latin America,* July 11, 1979, p. 223. (In 1979, P22.7 = US$1.)

[21] Holt, "Why the Bankers Suddenly Love Mexico," p. 140.

[22] *Ibid.,* p. 142.

FIGURE VI-1

Prices on the Bolsa de Valores, 1978-1979

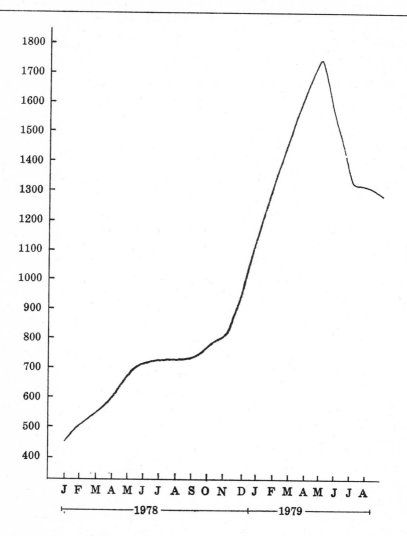

Source: Departamento de Análisis Bursátil, Banamex.

such as automotive and farm machinery industries, secondary petrochemicals, electronics, metals, pharmaceuticals, paper, and food processing; and the United States still provides the largest share (65-80 percent) of this investment.[23] Other foreign investment comes from West Germany, Japan, the United Kingdom, Canada, France, and Sweden. The list of multinational corporations that have planned new or expanded investment includes General Motors, Du Pont, Hitachi, Ford, Monsanto, Kimberly-Clark, Bayer, Dina-Renault, Volkswagen, and Chrysler.

Private investment in Mexico has been growing and, according to DIEMEX-Wharton EFA, is predicted to continue to increase through the 1980s (see Table A-2). Construction and capital goods industries lead the trend. A good illustration of the aggressive industrial development taking place in Mexico is the Monterrey Group, whose membership includes conglomerates such as the Grupo Industrial Alfa (steel production, land and resort development, mining, fibers, petrochemicals, electronics, plastics, and television); Grupo FIC (exporter of glass-related products and machinery); Valores Industriales—VISA (banking, food production, breweries, packaging, plastics, animal feeds, and prefabricated panels for housing); and the CYDSA (basic chemicals, acrylic fibers, and related products, plus packaging).

Business sources predicted that overall industrial production would increase by 10 percent in 1979 and in 1980.[24] PEMEX, the oil monopoly, leads all sectors in growth with oil output and petrochemical projects. Growth rates for individual economic sectors are presented in Table VI-1.

Although Mexico's oil reserves have captured the world's attention, huge mineral reserves have gone virtually unnoticed because of confiscatory tax policies that have impeded production. Investment in silver, copper, lead, zinc, and other basic chemicals accounts for the jump in the mining growth rate from 1978 to 1979. In the manufacturing sector, steel and automobiles largely contributed to the increase. The motor car industry, which lagged in 1976 and 1977, staged a dramatic turnabout in 1978. Chrysler de México led General Motors, Ford, and Volkswagen in sales for 1978, but that lead may be challenged because, in mid-1979,

---

[23] Business International Corporation, "Mexico," p. 4.

[24] "Business Outlook, Mexico," p. 229.

TABLE VI-1
Economic Growth by Sectors
Annual Rate of Change
(Percentage)

	1977	1978	1979	1980
GDP	3.2	6.6	7.3	6.6
Petroleum	15.9	16.9	18.5	27.7
Mining	0.9	—2.1	2.0	5.0
Manufacturing	3.6	8.5	9.1	5.2
Construction	—2.0	12.5	12.0	9.8
Electricity	7.7	10.1	8.8	6.6
Trade	2.0	4.7	6.1	4.6
Transportation and Communication	5.2	5.3	6.8	7.3
Agriculture	2.7	3.1	3.0	3.1
Others	2.1	4.6	4.2	4.3

Source: DIEMEX-Wharton EFA.

the major competitors announced investments in expansion projects.[25]

Despite the optimism regarding Mexico's economy, there are some inherent structural weaknesses that continue to plague the country. Unemployment and underemployment continue to be high. Some estimates place the figure as high as 50 percent.[26] Inflation in 1978 stood at 17.6 percent (see Table A-1) and, according to DIEMEX-Wharton EFA, is projected to increase. Mexico's capital goods requirements promise steadily mounting import bills, and the balance-of-trade deficit stood at $2.22 billion in 1978. An area of particular concern is the agricultural sector, which grew by only 3 percent in 1978. This sector still employs some 40 percent of the country's work force but accounts for only about 9 percent of the GDP. As pointed out in chapter III, agriculture's lack of growth is caused by the system of land tenure, which encourages the proliferation of small, inefficient, and non-irrigated plots; in addition, credit for investment in equipment

---

[25] Gerald F. Seib, "While Chrysler of U.S. Lags, its Mexican Unit Has Seized No. 1 Spot," *Wall Street Journal*, July 24, 1979, p. 1.

[26] Kevin Done and Hugh O'Shaughnessy, "Major increase in proven reserves," *Financial Times Survey*, August 30, 1979, p. 1.

and improved technology is lacking. Export crops such as tomatoes, strawberries, asparagus, coffee, and sugar assist the agricultural trade by providing $300 to $400 million, but in 1979, Mexico still had to import close to $1 billion in basic food items (chiefly corn and wheat).[27]

Economic-Industrial Policy

President López Portillo has been endeavoring to maintain a careful balance between development of Mexico's infrastructure and improvement in employment and controlling inflation. As stated by Miguel de la Madrid Hurtado, former treasury undersecretary and now the minister of planning and budgeting, "We are trying to get a steady rate of growth compatible with a diminishing rate of inflation." [28]

Funding for the administration's objectives of strengthening the infrastructure and bolstering employment will come from public, private, and foreign investment. Oil and gas exports alone will bring in revenues of close to $8 billion in 1980 and are projected to increase steadily (see Table A-3). President López Portillo recognizes that oil reserves permit better financing for development, but he intends to limit oil production so that the revenues may be more gradually absorbed by the economy. In his state of the nation address in September 1978, López Portillo said that oil strategy must avoid deforming Mexico's total productive structure.[29] It is expected that investment will go toward overhauling the railroad system; building new ports; increasing electrical generation capacity; upgrading the communications system; improving the water system, which in turn should benefit agriculture; and increasing steel production.

The administration's industrial development plan, which was drawn up by the secretary of national properties and industrial growth, José Andres de Oteyza, early in 1970,[30] is the cornerstone of Mexico's economic strategy. The forerunner of the plan was the government-sponsored Alliance for Production, which sought the support of business and labor to deal with problems affecting all sectors. The basis of the Alliance was the promotion of high-

---

[27] "Business Outlook, Mexico," p. 229.

[28] "Mexico's Reluctant Oil Boom," *Business Week*, January 15, 1979, p. 67.

[29] *Ibid.*, p. 64.

[30] "Mexico's Industrial Plan Plots the Course of a Daring Bid for Growth," *Business Latin America*, April 11, 1979, pp. 117-19.

volume, low-cost production of basic goods; the increase of employment; and the development of exports and markets.[31] The industrial development plan goes even further in designating incentives for investment and establishing priorities for regional development. The plan seeks to decentralize production facilities to promote the remote, rural areas over the Federal District and most of the states of Mexico, Monterrey, and Guadalajara, which are already highly developed areas. Decentralization, it is hoped, will accomplish yet another government objective—to stem rural migration to the overcrowded cities and to reduce illegal emigration to the United States.[32]

The development plan includes financial incentives, such as tax credits and fuel and raw materials discounts, that are designed to attract foreign investment. As in the past, however, investment will be on a minority share basis (except in the case of subsidiaries of foreign automakers) and is meant to "complement, rather than displace, local investment." [33] Generally, the plan has met with a favorable response, principally because it signals improvement in the government's management and sets forth clear priorities. The following criticisms, however, have been leveled against the plan: (1) the decentralized locations approved for government incentives may make transportation of raw materials and finished goods so costly as to offset the benefits; (2) companies will need closer dealings with the government to be certain of obtaining the promised incentives; and (3) the plan may end up as a blueprint for state investment, not private investment.[34]

López Portillo has been generally following a conservative, probusiness philosophy in his economic policies. He has controlled government spending, and his programs are aimed at heavy investment in industry to boost production and create employment rather than toward direct income redistribution. Furthermore, the president has obtained and, thus far, has been able to maintain labor's support in holding wage demands in check. It is not certain, however, how long labor will be patient as the cost of living escalates. The success of the less-than-inflation wage guide-

---

[31] Business International Corporation, "Mexico," p. 3.

[32] "Mexico's Industrial Plan Plots the Course," pp. 117-19; "New Mexican Incentives Give Forceful Support to Industrialization Plan," *Business Latin America*, April 18, 1979, pp. 122-25.

[33] Business International Corporation, "Mexico," p. 3.

[34] "Mexico's Development Plan Gets Mixed Reviews," *Business Latin America*, June 13, 1979, p. 189.

lines may in part depend on a voluntary price controls program begun in the private sector. The *Consejo Coordinador Empresarial*, the most important business organization in the country, has launched a "basic products program" that will control prices of some seventeen items, including beans, rice, coffee, and flour, which make up 55 percent of family expenditures.[35] Labor has expressed skepticism about the program, which it sees as an avoidance of mandatory price controls. Nevertheless, if the program proves effective, it would aid the fight against inflation and could keep labor demands under control.

With respect to monetary policy, the administration would clearly like to slow the growth of the money supply, but from all indications, this appears to be a very difficult goal to achieve. The targeted increase in the money supply for 1979 was set at 24 to 26 percent, but in the first two months of 1979, the money supply was 35 percent higher than for the same period in 1978.[36] The growth in the money supply has been largely fueled by oil revenues (see Table A-3) and is projected to continue throughout the near term. Therefore, it is likely that higher domestic interest rates and tighter credit will be features of the Mexican business climate, at least under the present administration.

OUTLOOK FOR PETROLEUM PRODUCTION AND EXPORTS

Foreign trade is projected to continue at a deficit through the 1980s (see Table A-3). Estimates show that the impressive increase in oil revenues and the impact of natural gas exports will still be offset by the growing demand for imported raw materials and capital goods.

According to PEMEX, Mexico will export 673,000 barrels of oil per day to the United States, or 87 percent of total crude oil exports, with the balance going to Israel and Spain.[37] Other buyers are rapidly lining up. Great Britain wants to trade North Sea crude for Mexican crude; France is to provide technical assistance on uranium development in return for exports of 100,000 barrels per day; and Japan is negotiating 220,000 barrels

---

[35] "Mexican private sector plans price limits," *Latin America Economic Report*, July 6, 1979, p. 206.

[36] "Mexico struggles to contain acceleration in growth," *Latin America Economic Report*, June 1, 1979, p. 165.

[37] Kevin Done, "Plenty of Would-be Buyers," *Financial Times Survey*, August 30, 1979, p. 4.

per day from 1980 in a package deal for construction of a supertanker port on Mexico's west coast.[38]

Pricing strategy, always a crucial issue, is predicted to follow the upward trend in world oil prices, and natural gas prices will not be far behind. The economic forecasts developed by Wharton EFA reflect the assumption of higher prices ($22.60 per barrel as of July 1, 1979, moderately rising to $25.00 by year-end, $26.00 in 1980, and $26.80 by 1981).[39]

Mexico has thus far resisted joining the Organization of Petroleum Exporting Countries, and indications are that it will not soon become a member. Informed observers note that, were the Arabs to impose another oil embargo on the West, the Mexicans would not participate; however, while Mexico is expected to continue to supply oil to the United States, it will be supplying that oil at the going price.[40]

The interesting question then becomes, how much and how fast? Although Mexico welcomes the improved investment and income outlook oil provides, there are certain problems associated with increased production. Chief among these are inflation, which has been aggravated by the oil revenues, and the problem of creating significantly more jobs (on the order of 800,000 per year, which the oil industry, by its capital-intensive nature, cannot itself provide). The level of investment in PEMEX will determine the rate of production, and Mexico intends to limit that production to a platform of 2.2 to 2.5 million barrels per day by 1980.[41]

LABOR OUTLOOK

Mexico's most pressing labor problems are the need for jobs and the continuing inflation eroding income. According to the president's state of the nation speech, only 28 percent of a population of 66.9 million in 1978 was "economically active"; however, it is estimated that almost 50 percent of the work force is

---

[38] James Flanigan, "Mexican Oil: The U.S. is most definitely not in the driver's seat," *Forbes*, January 22, 1979, p. 30.

[39] Wharton Econometric Forecasting Associates, Inc., "Mexican Econometric Model" (Philadelphia: WEFA, Inc., July 14, 1970), p. 3.

[40] Hugh O'Shaughnessy, "Oil Finds Revive Growth," *Financial Times*, January 3, 1979, p. 11.

[41] "Neighborliness is not enough," *Economist*, February 24, 1979, p. 36.

either unemployed or underemployed.[42] The Mexican labor force is also composed of young and politically active workers, who place intense pressure on the labor market; an estimated 800,000 enter the labor force each year.[43] Even illegal immigration of approximately 750,000 a year to the United States cannot absorb the overflow.[44]

Although the Mexican economy has become increasingly industrialized, about 40 percent of the population is still employed in the agricultural sector. In agriculture, particularly, underemployment is a problem because of a lack of opportunities in rural areas, the seasonal nature of the work, and the low wage rate. For employers in Mexico, the relatively low wage rate and the burgeoning population assure a cheap and plentiful labor supply. With the renewed industrial development, however, shortages of skilled labor and managerial personnel have been aggravated. A high turnover of well-paid technicians is common.[45] An amendment to the labor law, which calls for training programs to be established, may help this problem by increasing the number of skilled workers, but at best, this is a lengthy process.

Unions and Work Stoppages

The unions in Mexico remain very strong and are affiliated with the major political party, the PRI. Some 4 million, or about one-half of all industrial workers, are unionized and belong to one of the nine big national labor federations.[46] The strongest labor organization continues to be the CTM, led by Fidel Velázquez. As pointed out in chapter IV, the *Confederación Regional Obrera Mexicana* and the CTM are included in labor's political organization, the *Congreso del Trabajo;* and the leading opposition labor faction is the *Confederación Revolucionaria de Obreros y Campesinos.*

There are indications that, in the light of changing economic realities, Mexico's organized labor sector may be experiencing

---

[42] William Chislett, "The desperate search for work," *Financial Times,* November 2, 1978, p. 28; Done and O'Shaughnessy, "Major increase in proven reserves," p. 1.

[43] "Mexico's Reluctant Oil Boom," p. 65.

[44] "Mixed feelings about Mexico," *Economist,* December 30, 1978, p. 19.

[45] Business International Corporation, "Mexico," p. 22.

[46] *Ibid.*

increasing pressures in the form of challenges to traditional leadership. First, there has been wide speculation regarding future CTM leadership. According to trade unionist sources, Fidel Velázquez will run for another term in the spring of 1980,[47] and therefore, no successor has been designated. The Velázquez leadership, however, has been challenged by dissension from within and by outside pressure from the independent unions. In May 1978, the CTM refused to support an affiliated union that was striking against the La Caridad copper mine. The stoppage occurred because the workers wanted better living conditions and also demanded the right to disaffiliate from the CTM. The strike, involving 5,700 workers, lasted for forty-four days, and the CTM retaliated by backing the company and even advised that the army be called in.[48] After the troops arrived, the strike was called off, and none of the workers' demands were negotiated. The company, a joint venture including the Nacional Financiera; the Comisión de Fomento Minero; private Mexican interests; and Asarco, an American company, gained permission to lay off almost one-half of the work force when production began.

In July 1978, Velázquez's recognized leadership in the *Congreso del Trabajo* was tested by the presence of the independent *Federación de Sindicatos de Trabajadores Universitarios* at the national assembly. This group had never before been included in the *Congreso,* and it was allegedly against Velázquez's wishes that it was there. Another independent, the *Frente Auténtico del Trabajo,* a state of Mexico group, challenged CTM jurisdiction at Searle, General Electric, Spicer, and other companies. "A similar jurisdictional problem caused slowdowns and eventually a change in union leadership at state-owned Telefonos de Mexico, and the Federal Electricity Commission had to summon the army to fend off strikes threatened by a union splinter group." [49]

Other affiliates, such as the powerful *Sindicato de Trabajadores Petroleros de la República Mexicana* (STPRM), are demonstrating increasingly dissident and independent tendencies. There have been demands for greater democratization not only in the government party (PRI) but also in the union structure itself,

---

[47] Author's conversation with Mexican trade unionist, August 2, 1979.

[48] "Mexican union breaks miners' strike," *Latin America Economic Report,* May 19, 1978, p. 152.

[49] Business International Corporation, "Mexico," p. 23.

as well as demands for more labor representatives in the Mexican congress.[50] Therefore, it appears that independents are gaining strength with supporters in such key areas as the universities, the steel and auto industries, the subway system, and the telephone company.[51]

Wages

The unions are increasingly dissatisfied with the control on wages instituted under the López Portillo administration. In an effort to slow inflation, the government limited wage increases in 1977 to 10 percent; in 1978, to 12 to 13 percent; and in 1979 settlements, to 15 percent.[52] Regional commissions made up of government, employer, and union representatives set minimum wages for over 111 separate labor market areas.[53] Skills, as well as geographic region, determine wage differentials. Wages in unionized industries are negotiated through collective bargaining, are in general higher than the legal minimum, and are often subject to an additional premium of about 50 to 60 percent for legally required fringe benefits.[54]

Working Hours

In Mexico, the normal workday has been eight hours, and the normal workweek, forty-eight hours. After every six-day work interval, the worker is entitled to one day of rest with full pay. Overtime is paid at twice the normal rate for the first nine hours a week and at triple pay thereafter; a 25 percent premium is paid for Sunday work.[55]

There has been considerable union pressure to lower the workweek to forty hours for all industries. Employers have resisted because lowering the workweek has the effect of raising wages. Likewise, it is felt that productivity will suffer. The trend, however, seems to be moving toward the shorter week. Reportedly,

---

50 "Dissenters challenge power of Mexican union leader," *Latin America Economic Report*, July 21, 1978, p. 223.

51 Alan Riding, "Mexican Troops Help End Strikes by Labor Rebels," *New York Times*, July 31, 1978, p. A-3.

52 Author's conversation with Mexican trade unionist, August 2, 1979.

53 Lowenstern, *Profile of Labor Conditions: Mexico*, p. 6.

54 Business International Corporation, "Mexico," p. 23.

55 *Ibid.*

the rubber industry was the first to go on the forty-hour week (in 1975). Some individual companies, such as Ford and General Motors, are also on the shorter week, and others are phasing in the reduction.[56] Workers for PEMEX have been on the shorter week since 1973, as have employees of the Social Security Institute. Although supporting the forty-hour week in the PRI platform for 1976-1982, the government has allowed the matter to be decided by individual industries' collective bargaining.

INTERNATIONAL TRADE SECRETARIAT ACTIVITIES

The Mexican unions remain active to varying degrees in the international trade secretariats (ITSs). There have been no disaffiliations, although occasionally a union may be claimed by more than one ITS. No major meetings of secretariats occurred in Mexico, nor were there claims of ITS actions concerning Mexican affiliates during the three years 1977-1979. The most active of the secretariats in Mexican matters were the International Federation of Commercial, Clerical and Technical Employees (FIET), the International Metalworkers' Federation (IMF), and the Postal, Telegraph and Telephone International (PTTI).

The Health and Social Security Sector of the FIET held a seminar in Mexico from June 3 to 7, 1978, with representatives from all Spanish-speaking affiliates in attendance. In September 1978, FIET representatives attended a meeting of the International Confederation of Free Trade Unions (ICFTU) in Cuernavaca, Mexico, to discuss strengthening cooperation between the ICFTU and the *Organización Regional Interamericana de Trabajadores*, the Latin American regional organization.[57]

The IMF continues to be active in Mexico. The regional office in Mexico City maintains close relations with unions in the CTM, particularly those in the electrical manufacturing industry, and with some other unions that are members of other confederations, such as the Olivetti union and shipbuilding and aluminum workers. In March 1977, the Sole Union of Electrical Workers of Mexico (SUTERM), an affiliate of the CTM with approximately eleven thousand members, held a training seminar for its

---

[56] *Ibid.*

[57] *FIET Newsletter*, July-August 1978, p. 7; *ibid.*, September 1978, p. 6.

officers in the electronics sector under the sponsorship of the CTM, the IMF, and the International Labour Organisation.[58] The PTTI, in conjunction with and underwritten by the Friedrich Ebert Foundation, held a special multinational seminar in Mexico in October 1978 to study the subject of industrial democracy. The PTTI's Mexican affiliate, the *Sindicato de Telefonistas de la República Mexicana* (STRM), made a presentation at the seminar. Later, at the Twenty-third World Congress of the PTTI, the results of that seminar were made public. In April 1979, the STRM sent a delegate to the international seminar on consumer cooperatives, held in Bogotá, Colombia.[59]

MEXICO'S FUTURE

The conclusions that may be drawn from the preceding discussion are generally positive for Mexico's economic vitality, political stability, and labor outlook. In his state of the nation address in September 1979, President López Portillo stressed the favorable atmosphere for continued industrial growth in a context of attention to social welfare objectives. The subsidy policy, directed toward holding down prices of basic goods and coupled with tax incentives for industry, received special emphasis and represents an important commitment on the part of the administration.

With regard to labor policies, President López Portillo announced that the period of "unilateral sacrifice" is now over.[60] Wage increases can be expected along with increases in fringe benefits, union stores, and low-cost basic goods. Taken together, these moves are aimed at reestablishing the purchasing power of workers. The administration has also identified worker training programs as a priority, along with a policy of rural development designed to stem the tide of illegal emigration to the United States and migration to Mexico's already overcrowded cities. Other social goals that the president articulated include expanded medical care and an increase in the scope of the social security system, education, and population control.

---

[58] IMF, *Report of Activities to the 24th World Congress, Munich, 24-28 October, 1977*, Vol. 1 (Geneva, 1977), p. 103; *ibid.*, Vol. 2, p. 22.

[59] Based on reports of the various secretariats.

[60] "López Portillo stresses aggressive growth for Mexican economy," *Business Latin America*, September 5, 1979, p. 283.

In relations with the rest of the world, and with the United States in particular, Mexico has exhibited a more aggressive role. The negotiations for the nation's oil and natural gas resources have illustrated Mexico's more confident position. The real challenge to Mexico is whether it can translate this confidence into achievement. Mexico has many complex problems with which it still must deal, such as population control and development of the infrastructure. The years ahead will demonstrate whether it has the leadership that can effectively tackle those problems and therefore place Mexico firmly on the path from a developing to a developed nation.

APPENDIXES

Appendix A

WHARTON ECONOMETRIC FORECASTS FOR MEXICO

The following projections were computed by Wharton Econometric Forecasting Associates, Inc. (EFA), the first econometric research institution to generate regular forecasts for less-developed countries. In addition to projections for Mexico, Wharton EFA also makes Brazilian forecasts based upon another highly sophisticated econometric model. The group has participated in the development of models for Panama, Puerto Rico, Venezuela, and Spain.

The Wharton EFA Mexican Econometric Model currently has the support of more than sixty Mexican and American corporations and Mexican government agencies, which receive four forecast updates a year and meet twice a year to discuss the projections and model development. The Mexican Econometric Model forecasts through the year 1990.[1]

Readers interested in obtaining additional information regarding these projections may contact Abel Beltrán del Río, Director of Latin American Projects, Wharton Econometric Forecasting Associates, Inc., 3624 Science Center, Philadelphia, Pennsylvania 19104, U.S.A.

---

[1] For the purposes of this study, projections have been used through 1985. The data were compiled and interpreted under the guidance of Enrique Sánchez, Economist, Wharton EFA.

173

TABLE A-1
Mexican Model Control Solution—July 14, 1979
New Crude Oil Export Prices and Delayed Achievement of Oil Export Targets

Main Indicators	1978	1979	1980	1981
Population (millions)	66.94	69.15	71.39	73.46
Gross Domestic Product (GDP) (percentage)	6.6	7.3	6.6	8.7
General Inflation Rate GDP Deflator (percentage)	17.9	18.8	18.6	17.5
Consumer Price Index (percentage)	17.4	18.9	21.1	18.5
Money Supply (billions of pesos)	258.07	319.83	443.19	569.99
Percent Change	31.7	31.7	30.4	28.6
Exchange Rate (pesos per U.S. dollar)	22.77	23.30	24.80	25.72
Total Employment (millions)	17.64	18.27	18.95	19.66
Percent Change	3.4	3.6	3.8	3.7
Labor Productivity	24.75	25.64	26.34	27.61
Percent Change	3.1	3.6	2.7	4.8
Unit Labor Cost—National Average	1,412.39	1,615.37	1,875.86	2,179.83
Percent Change	15.4	14.4	16.1	16.2
Average Annual Wage Rate (thousands of pesos)	34.96	41.42	49.41	60.19
Percent Change	15.1	18.5	19.3	21.8

TABLE A-1 (continued)

Main Indicators	1982	1983	1984	1985
Population (millions)	75.59	77.79	80.04	82.36
Gross Domestic Product (GDP) (percentage)	7.8	4.7	7.3	7.8
General Inflation Rate GDP Deflator (percentage)	15.8	14.2	14.2	14.0
Consumer Price Index (percentage)	17.0	16.7	14.8	14.5
Money Supply (billions of pesos)	706.24	852.13	1,061.54	1,319.12
Percent Change	23.9	20.7	24.6	24.3
Exchange Rate (pesos per U.S. dollar)	25.72	25.72	25.72	25.72
Total Employment (millions)	20.50	21.24	21.84	22.64
Percent Change	4.3	3.6	2.8	3.7
Labor Productivity	28.55	28.84	30.09	31.28
Percent Change	3.4	1.0	4.3	4.0
Unit Labor Cost—National Average	2,533.18	2,929.97	3,328.81	3,782.47
Percent Change	16.2	15.6	13.7	13.6
Average Annual Wage Rate (thousands of pesos)	72.34	84.49	100.16	118.31
Percent Change	20.2	16.8	18.6	18.1

Source: DIEMEX-Wharton EFA.

TABLE A-2

Final Demand in Real 1960 Pesos

Mexican Model Control Solution—July 14, 1979

New Crude Oil Export Prices and Delayed Achievement of Oil Export Targets

(Billions)

Components of Final Demand	1978	1979	1980	1981
Gross Domestic Product	436.53	468.33	499.28	542.75
Total Consumption	338.21	361.34	381.12	406.39
Private Consumption	291.53	310.60	327.08	348.14
Government Consumption	46.68	50.74	54.04	58.25
Gross Fixed Investment	91.48	106.84	122.10	136.91
Private Gross Fixed Investment	50.74	59.34	68.23	76.74
Government Gross Fixed Investment	40.74	47.50	53.87	60.17
In Petroleum and Gas	12.99	13.44	12.90	9.28
In Other Sectors	27.74	34.06	40.97	50.89

	1982	1983	1984	1985
Gross Domestic Product	585.23	612.52	657.09	708.27
Total Consumption	434.14	460.92	492.21	525.90
Private Consumption	371.17	393.47	419.10	446.87
Government Consumption	62.97	67.44	73.11	79.03
Gross Fixed Investment	149.91	154.34	170.36	189.16
Private Gross Fixed Investment	83.24	85.33	91.90	99.64
Government Gross Fixed Investment	66.67	69.00	78.46	89.52
In Petroleum and Gas	9.60	8.07	12.99	13.44
In Other Sectors	57.07	60.93	65.47	76.07

Source: DIEMEX-Wharton EFA.

Note: In 1960, P12.49 = US$1.

TABLE A-3
Export-Import Summary
Mexican Model Control Solution—July 14, 1979
New Crude Oil Export Prices and Delayed Achievement of Oil Export Targets
(Current US$ Billions)

	1978	1979	1980	1981	1982	1983	1984	1985
Total Exports of Goods, Services, and Factors	10.69	14.42	19.20	24.40	29.03	31.95	36.43	42.58
Total Merchandise	5.83	8.72	12.77	16.98	20.67	22.46	25.84	30.58
Petroleum	1.80	4.27	7.29	10.26	12.41	13.33	15.66	18.50
Natural Gas	0.00	0.00	0.58	1.24	2.26	2.57	2.90	4.00
Other Goods	4.03	4.45	4.90	5.48	6.00	6.56	7.28	8.08
Silver Production	0.24	0.27	0.32	0.38	0.45	0.54	0.64	0.75
Services and Border Trade	3.85	4.59	5.17	5.98	6.72	7.62	8.47	9.58
Factors of Production	0.77	0.85	0.95	1.06	1.19	1.33	1.49	1.67
Total Imports of Goods, Services, and Factors	13.15	17.36	20.84	24.58	28.93	32.89	37.62	43.95
Total Goods	8.05	10.87	13.39	16.12	19.28	22.13	25.55	30.20
Consumption Goods	1.40	1.76	2.08	2.42	2.87	3.35	3.80	4.42
Production Goods	6.65	9.11	11.31	13.70	16.41	18.78	21.75	25.78
Services and Border Trade	2.30	2.92	3.45	4.05	4.80	5.41	6.05	6.92
Factors of Production	2.80	3.57	4.00	4.42	4.86	5.36	6.08	6.83
Balance and Goods Services and Factors	−2.46	−2.94	−1.64	−0.18	−0.11	−0.94	−1.19	−1.37

Source: DIEMEX-Wharton EFA.

Appendix B

UNION SURVEY SOURCES

The survey of international trade secretariat activities in Mexico presented in Table IV-6 is based upon the following sources:

INTERNATIONAL FEDERATION OF BUILDING AND WOODWORKERS (IFBWW)

John Löfbald, IFBWW general secretary, to the author, June 28, 1976.

INTERNATIONAL FEDERATION OF CHEMICAL, ENERGY AND GENERAL WORKERS (ICEF)

16th Statutory Congress, 27-29 October 1976, Montreal: Executive Committee; Activities Report of the Secretary General; List of Membership (Geneva: ICF, 1976).

ICF Bulletin, 15th Congress (1973).

ICF Bulletin, January-February 1972.

14th Statutory Congress, 22-24 October 1970, Copenhagen: Congress Reports, 2 vols. (Geneva: ICF, 1970).

In addition to the above, the Industrial Research Unit has investigated and checked nearly every claim of ICEF solidarity action since 1969; nearly all have been found to be more imagined than real. See the following articles by Herbert R. Northrup and Richard L. Rowan: "Multinational Union Activity in the 1976 U.S. Rubber Tire Strike," *Sloan Management Review*, Vol. 18, No. 3 (Spring 1977), pp. 17-28; "Multinational Bargaining Approaches in the Western European Flat Glass Industry," *Industrial and Labor Relations Review*, Vol. 30 (October 1976), pp. 32-46; "The ICF-IFPCW Conflict," *Columbia Journal of World Business*, Vol. IX (Winter 1974), pp. 109-120; and "Multinational Collective Bargaining Activity: The Factual Record in Chemicals, Glass, and Rubber Tires," *Columbia Journal of World Business*, Vol. IX (Summer 1974), pp. 49-63 and (Spring 1974), pp. 112-124.

178

INTERNATIONAL FEDERATION OF COMMERCIAL, CLERICAL AND TECHNICAL EMPLOYEES (FIET)

FIET Newsletter, Nos. 1-15 (1974)

Report on Activities and Financial Report Covering the Period from 1970 to 1973 (Geneva: FIET, 1973).

Report on Activities and Financial Report Covering the Period from 1967 to 1970 (Geneva: FIET, 1970).

INTERNATIONAL GRAPHIC FEDERATION (IGF)

Heinz Göke, IGF general secretary, to the author, July 13, 1976.

INTERNATIONAL UNION OF FOOD AND ALLIED WORKERS' ASSOCIATIONS (IUF)

"Regional Activities—Latin America," 18th Congress, Geneva, Switzerland, 24-28 January 1977. (Mimeographed.)

IUF News Bulletin, 1973-1975.

"Documents of the Secretariat," 17th Congress, Geneva, Switzerland, 29-30 January 1973. (Mimeographed.)

Meetings of the Executive and Managing Committee (Geneva: IUF, 1970).

INTERNATIONAL METALWORKERS' FEDERATION (IMF)

Metal, Bulletin of the International Metalworkers' Federation (Mexico) Vol. XVII (1977).

Crisis or Change (Geneva: IMF, 1975).

Twenty-third World Congress, Stockholm, 2-6 July 1974, 2 vols. (Geneva: IMF, 1974).

Resolutions Adopted at the 23rd Congress of the International Metalworkers' Federation, Stockholm 1974 (Geneva: IMF, 1974).

Bulletin of the International Metalworkers' Federation, No. 38 (October 1971).

INTERNATIONAL FEDERATION OF PLANTATION, AGRICULTURAL AND ALLIED WORKERS (IFPAAW)

IFPAAW Snips, Nos. 5-11 (1976) ; Nos. 1-3 (1977).

Tom S. Bavin, IFPAAW secretary general, to the author, July 16, 1976.

Fourth World Congress (Geneva: IFPAAW, 1976).

Proceedings of the Third World Congress of the IFPAAW (Geneva: IFPAAW, 1971).

Report of the Secretariat, IFPAAW Third World Congress (Geneva: IFPAAW, 1971).

Report of the Secretariat, IFPAAW Second World Congress (Geneva: IFPAAW, 1965).

POSTAL, TLELGRAPH AND TELEPHONE INTERNATIONAL (PTTI)

Departmento de Estudios e Informaciones Laborales, *La International del Personal de Correos, Telegrafos y Telefonos en las Americas* (Washington, D.C.: PTTI, 1976).

Departmento de Estudios e Informaciones Laborales, *Las Condiciones de Trabajo en America Latina* (Washington, D.C.: PTTI, 1976).

INTERNATIONAL TRANSPORT WORKERS' FEDERATION (ITF)

XXXII Congress, Dublin, 21-29 July 1977: Report on Activities—1974-1975-1976 (London: ITF, 1977).

Harold Lewis, ITF assitant general secretary, to the author, June 29, 1976.

ITF Newsletter (London), Nos. 9-12 (1973) ; Nos. 1-12 (1974) ; Nos. 1-12 (1975) ; Nos. 1-5 (1976).

XXXI Congress, Stockholm, 7-15 August 1974: Report on Activities—1971-1972-1973 (London: ITF, 1974).

ITF Journal (London), Vol. 31, Nos. 2-3 (1971) ; Vol. 33, Nos. 1-3 (1973) ; Vol. 34, Nos. 1-3 (1974).

Transporte (Lima), Vol. 17, Nos. 1-2 (Enero-Abril 1973).

XXX Congress, Vienna, 28 July—6 August 1971: Report on Activities for the years 1968, 1969 and 1970 (London: ITF, 1971).

Proceedings of the 29th Congress, Wiesbaden, 28 July—3 August 1968. (London: ITF, 1968).

International Transport Workers' Federation (London: ITF, n.d.). (Leaflet.)

Index

The reader should consult chapter VI for
1977-80 developments concerning the entries below.

STUDIES OF NEGRO EMPLOYMENT

Order from the Industrial Research Unit
The Wharton School, University of Pennsylvania
Philadelphia, Pennsylvania 19104

* Order these books from University Microfilms, Inc., Attn: Books Editorial Department, 300 North Zeeb Road, Ann Arbor, Michigan 48106.